Michael Mann

CONSCIOUSNESS AND ACTION AMONG THE WESTERN WORKING CLASS

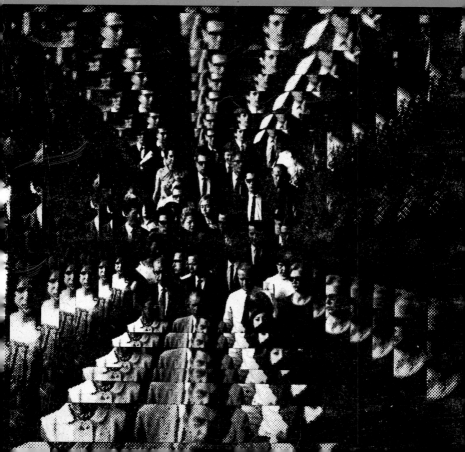

STUDIES IN SOCIOLOGY

This series, prepared under the auspices of the British Sociological Association, is designed to provide short but comprehensive and scholarly treatments of key problem-areas in sociology. The books do not offer summary accounts of the current state of research in various fields, but seek rather to analyse matters which are the subject of controversy or debate. The series is designed to cover a broad range of topics, falling into three categories: (1) abstract problems of social theory and social philosophy; (2) interpretative questions posed by the writings of leading social theorists; (3) issues in empirical sociology. In addition, the series will carry translations of important writings in sociology which have not previously been available in English. Each book makes a substantive contribution to its particular topic, while at the same time giving the reader an indication of the main problems at issue; each carries an annotated bibliography, comprising a critical survey of relevant further literature.

ANTHONY GIDDENS

University of Cambridge

STUDIES IN SOCIOLOGY

General Editor: ANTHONY GIDDENS
Editorial Advisers: T. B. BOTTOMORE, DAVID LOCKWOOD and
ERNEST GELLNER

Published

THE SOCIOLOGY OF SOCIAL MOVEMENTS
J. A. Banks

POLITICS AND SOCIOLOGY IN THE THOUGHT OF MAX WEBER
Anthony Giddens

PROFESSIONS AND POWER
Terence J. Johnson

CONSCIOUSNESS AND ACTION AMONG THE WESTERN WORKING CLASS
Michael Mann

THE SOCIAL PROCESS OF INNOVATION: A STUDY IN THE SOCIOLOGY
OF SCIENCE
M. J. Mulkay

Forthcoming

MARXIST SOCIOLOGY
T. B. Bottomore

MATHEMATICS AND SOCIOLOGY
B. Hindess

STRIKES AND INDUSTRIAL CONFLICT
G. Ingham

THE DEVELOPMENT OF THE SOCIOLOGY OF KNOWLEDGE
S. Lukes

MICHELS AND THE CRITIQUE OF SOCIAL DEMOCRACY
F. Parkin

Consciousness and Action among the Western Working Class

MICHAEL MANN
Lecturer in Sociology, University of Essex

Macmillan

First published 1973 by
THE MACMILLAN PRESS LTD
London and Basingstoke
Associated companies in New York Toronto
Dublin Melbourne Johannesburg and Madras

SBN 333 13773 6

Printed in Great Britain by
THE ANCHOR PRESS LTD
Tiptree, Essex

CONTENTS

PREFACE

This short book originated in a research project on international differences in factory social structure, in which I participated in 1967 and 1968 as a member of a Cambridge University research team, together with groups from Columbia University, New York and the Universities of Munich, Paris and Turin. After one year, supported by grant GS–1685 of the National Science Foundation, our own international differences proved too great for us to continue. However, I am grateful to my then colleagues for stimulating my interest in these problems. For their helpful criticisms of earlier drafts of this essay I wish also to thank Colin Bell, Peter Burgess, Anthony Giddens, John Goldthorpe, David Lockwood, Jill Mann, Sandy Stewart and Maryse and Pierre Tripier.

M. M.

1. INTRODUCTION

The main disadvantage of asking the question, 'Is the working class still a force for revolutionary change in the West?', is that most readers will already have decided on an answer. Yet the nature of this answer will vary according to the reader's political persuasion and nationality. Whereas Marxists and many Frenchmen and Italians might be inclined to answer 'yes', those to the political Right and to the north-west (in Britain and the United States especially) are more likely to answer 'no'. Clearly, both groups cannot be correct, though each may be reflecting accurately a segment of the reality of the West today. For, whereas a proletarian revolution seems inconceivable in the United States, only slightly less so in Western Germany and improbable in Great Britain, in France and Italy it appears a distinct possibility, as the dramatic events of May–June 1968 showed. Hence this book has a comparative focus, on class conflict in Britain, France, Italy and the United States, concentrating especially on the first two countries. All of these countries are capitalist liberal democracies, at a more or less comparable level of overall technological development and with identifiably 'Western' cultural values. Why then the apparent differences between their class relations?

There are two conventional though opposed ways of interpreting these differences coming from the 'Right' and from the 'Left' of modern class theory—respectively, *the end of ideology thesis* and *Marxism*. Whereas the former views class conflict as decreasing with the development of mature capitalist societies, the latter predicts its increase. Their mutual confidence in predicting comes from a shared quality of economic determinism. Both view the economic process as determining the structure of modern societies, but one sees this as producing class compromise, the other conflict and revolution.

9

By the label 'end of ideology theorists' I describe those American writers, loosely connected with each other and with functionalism, who analysed in the 1950s and 1960s what they saw as a secular and continuing decline in socialist ideology among most of the Western working class. The principal figures were Daniel Bell, Clark Kerr and S. M. Lipset, while much of the detailed research was carried out at the Berkeley Institute of Industrial Relations. Their writings differed, particularly in the extent to which they were willing to predict boldly the future of the West, but it is possible to construct from their themes an 'artificial end of ideology' theory. Its central tenet would be that there is an inherent strain in the industrialisation process toward the compromise of class interests and the institutionalisation of conflict. For Clark Kerr and his collaborators (1962) this is even part of the 'logic' of industrialisation. Unlike Marxists, they see the conflict between capital and labour as being essentially a quantitative economic dispute about 'who should get how much' of the surplus. And for some of them a rising standard of prosperity is itself conducive to a decline in conflict. The general view of the group is that, though economic conflict cannot be eliminated, it can be channelled into compromise bargaining which then reinforces its own precondition, the growth of the surplus available for distribution. In this way conflict becomes *functional*. Thus, for example, the militancy of American trade unions is regarded as pressurising management into cost-reduction and greater efficiency, to the potential benefit of both capital and labour. Institutionalisation also isolates each type of conflict from other types, and class conflict is fragmented into separate industrial, political, etc., disputes. 'Class' conflict consequently does not threaten social stability and may be actually functional for the existing structure of society. In this way the economic determinism of Marxism has been turned against itself, and most 'end of ideology' theorists paint the institutionalised politics and the industrial relations of the West in fairly rosy colours. It should also be noted that phenomena such as work deprivation or alienation rarely appear in their analyses, and we are generally left with the impression that the working class is reasonably content with its role in existing society.

These writers are well aware that some Western countries still

10

exhibit an apparently high level of class conflict. But they argue that this is caused by extra-industrial elements of society. France and Italy are their normal examples, and the turbulence of French and Italian class relations are attributed to such factors as 'dynastic' or traditional-minded *élites*, a religion which disparages economic activity and a labour force recently uprooted from a rural setting. As Lipset expresses it, class conflict there is 'a function of the extent to which the enduring economic struggle among the classes overlapped with the issues concerning the place of religion and the traditional status structure' (Lipset 1964, p. 272; cf. also Ross and Hartman 1960; Kerr *et al*. 1962). And the persistent economic determinism of these writers generally leads them to predict, more or less boldly, that 'tradition' will give way before the modernising, secular, urban and democratic influence of industry and thus precipitate a decline in class conflict and in the ideology of socialism (among the working class). From 'the end of ideology' perspective, therefore, we would conclude that severe class conflict is a product of extra-industrial elements of society and will decline with further industrialisation.

Marxism would naturally lead us to opposite conclusions. In contrasting the two, we should note firstly that the key term in each theory differs: while 'the end of ideology' theorists speak of 'industrialism', Marxists speak of 'capitalism'. This indicates that they posit not only different outcomes, but also different causes, of the development of Western societies. What one sees as the peculiar effects of capitalism, the other sees as common to all processes of industrialisation. This wide-ranging controversy, the 'Marx versus Weber' legacy, is for the most part outside the scope of this essay, however, and I will use only an operational definition of capitalism here.

It seems useful to describe modern Western societies as capitalist because in them the worker typically sells his labour power in a formally free market and thereby places himself under the control of those responsible to the provider of capital for the enterprise. But in this short book I can make no claim as to whether the good and the ills of the working class in contemporary society are to be attributed to capitalism. This limitation ought to be emphasised in the case of 'alienation', by which I shall refer to

11

the psychological state of 'abasement and indignation' (to use Marx's terms) resulting from the selling (alienating) of one's labour power—whether or not this is peculiar to capitalism. This is a narrower conception of alienation than Marx's own, and it prevents me from examining his theory in its entirety.

Yet much remains contentious even if we do not penetrate far into the origins of Western social structure. Three main strands of contemporary Marxism appear relevant: 'subjective' versus 'objective' views of class, the theory of 'the new working class', and theories of uneven development and over-determination.

The first of these is a false problem which I can quickly dispose of. Many Marxists today argue that whereas the 'objective' conditions for a proletarian revolution exist or are relatively advanced, the workers' 'subjective' consciousness of their historic role lags behind. Theories of 'false consciousness', or references to Lenin's supposed belief that the working class can generate only trade-union consciousness, normally make an appearance here. Yet regardless of whether this is a correct interpretation of Lenin's position (see Hyman 1971) it is a strange kind of Marxism, for it lacks the very essence of the materialist dialectic, the relation between theory and practice. According to Marx himself, the consciousness of the proletariat emerges from its direct and practical experience of the fundamental contradiction between the existing individualist relations of production and the emerging collective forces of production. While capitalist relations are based on individual private property, the productive forces develop a proletariat whose power is collectively based and experienced. Working-class consciousness grows dialectically, therefore, with experience in trade unions, in political parties and in the sphere of production itself. Hence, according to Marx, if subjective consciousness is lacking, so too are the objective conditions, for the two cannot exist separately. I will, therefore, ignore the subjective versus objective debate, and hypothesise that class consciousness is a dialectical process.

Yet Marxists are characteristically somewhat vague about the nature of this dialectical process. Sorel's definition of dialectics as the art of reconciling opposites by means of mumbo-jumbo springs to mind in this connection. We must approach the Marxist conception of working-class consciousness with more circumspection than is conventional. It is necessary to distinguish clearly between the four main elements implied in the conception.

Firstly, we can separate class *identity*—the definition of oneself as working-class, as playing a distinctive role in common with other workers in the productive process. Secondly comes class *opposition*—the perception that the capitalist and his agents constitute an enduring opponent to oneself. These two elements interact dialectically; that is to say opposition itself serves to reinforce identity, and vice-versa. Thirdly is class *totality*—the acceptance of the two previous elements as the defining characteristics of (*a*) one's total social situation and (*b*) the whole society in which one lives. Finally comes the conception of an *alternative* society, a goal toward which one moves through the struggle with the opponent. True revolutionary consciousness is the combination of all four, and an obviously rare occurrence. Marxism provides a theory of escalation of consciousness from the first to the fourth. Consciousness grows (some Marxists say it 'explodes') as the worker links his own concrete experience to an analysis of wider structures and then to alternative structures. It is in this sense that Marxism is a materialist theory : contradictions within the sphere of production and the growth of collective power are experienced by the worker before he generalises a theory of socialism. The extent to which, and the conditions under which, this dialectical process occurs in reality is the main subject of this essay.

The second strand of contemporary Marxism, the theory of the 'new working class', draws attention to the ambiguities found within classical Marxism concerning the nature of the workers' potential form of social organisation, their *collective labour power*. Are we to view this power as based on the sheer weight of numbers of a massified working class, or is it a power emanating from the developing nature of production in advanced capitalism? In the former case, the mass of the working population is placed in a class position at work similar to that in which they participate as part of a working-class community outside. They are impelled to revolution by a sense of common exploitation and alienation. This has been the traditional Marxist prediction. Unfortunately, it leaves unexplained the goal of the revolution— why should it be toward socialism and communism, unless 'the people' have an inherent drive toward collectivism? This formulation tends to leave out the distinctively Marxian concern with the 'progressive' aspects of the forces of production, which is the key to Marx's view of social change as a whole. It is not merely that 'the mass of misery, oppression, slavery, degradation, exploitation' grows, but also that the 'centralisation of the means of production and socialisation of labour at last reach a point where they become incompatible with their capitalist integument' (*Capital* I, p. 763). With the recent circulation of Marx's *Grundrisse*, this interpretation has received a new twist in this vital passage:

> To the degree that large-scale industry develops, the creation of real wealth comes to depend less on labor-time and on the quantity of labor expended, and more on the power of the instruments which are set in motion during labor-time . . . labor no longer appears as an integral element of the productive process; rather man acts as supervisor and regulator of the productive process itself. . . . He stands at the side of the productive process, instead of being its chief actor. With this transformation, the cornerstone of production and wealth is neither the labor which man directly expends, nor the time he spends at work, but rather the appropriation of his own collective power, his understanding of nature and his mastery of nature, exercised by him as a social body—in short it is the development of the social individual. (Quoted and commented on by Nicolaus 1968.)

Hence a more truly Marxian formulation might well be that the socialistic nature of the proletarian revolution is guaranteed by workers' direct experience of the emerging necessity to organise production collectively, and that their *distinctive* power is not weight of numbers but rather the actual exercise of collective co-ordination and control in advanced production *before* the revolution.

This is no mere dispute of scholarship, for it involves the fundamental questions of 'When might the revolution occur?' and 'Who might make it?' This new interpretation might lead us to locate a revolution in technologically advanced capitalist societies rather than in the nineteenth century, with the principal actors being not unskilled, alienated labourers, but skilled and self-confident workers and technicians. We must take very seriously, therefore, recent theories of 'post-industrial society' and 'the new working class', formulated in France and appearing to receive some support in the events of May–June 1968.

The third Marxist strand can be traced from certain elements of Marx's own writing, through the experience of the Bolsheviks in 1917, to recent French theories of *uneven development* and *over-determination*. It constitutes a consistent attempt to formulate a Marxist theory of *multi-causality*. Here, for example, is Trotsky's account of 1917 :

> If the agrarian problem, as a heritage from the barbarism of the old Russian history, had been solved by the bourgeoisie, if it could have been solved by them, the Russian proletariat could not possibly have come to power in 1917. In order to realise the Soviet state, there was required a drawing together and mutual penetration of the factors belonging to completely different historic species : a peasant war—that is, a movement characteristic of the dawn of bourgeois development—and a proletarian insurrection, the movement signalising its decline. That is the essence of 1917. (1967 edn, p. 64.)

This is still a distinctively Marxist interpretation, for Trotsky considers the development of the productive forces to be the principal determinant of the revolution. Yet if development is highly uneven, social structure will not correspond to the more widespread Marxist model of a two-class mature capitalist society presented, for example, in *Capital*. Trotsky's (and Lenin's) emphasis on unevenness as a cause of revolution seems especially relevant today to an analysis of class conflict in France and Italy. Just as the complex and unstable political relations between the Russian tsar, foreign capital, the native bourgeoisie, proletariat, landlords, rich peasants and poor peasants contributed to the revolutions of 1917, might not those in France, for example, between an interventionist State, paternalist employers, divided bourgeoisie and the 'new' and 'old' working class have similar consequences?

15

Such an analogy might seem to lead to a somewhat unorthodox Marxism of 'exceptional social situations'. Yet, as Althusser has asked, are we not always in exceptional situations with respect to the pure and abstract contradiction between Capital and Labour? Where this contradiction appears is it not always surrounded by local historical circumstances? Althusser attempts to formulate a theory of such peculiarities by grafting his concept of *over-determination* on to theories of uneven development.

The starting-point is Engels's famous letter in which he expressed reservations about economic determinism and argued that the economic base determines social structure 'only in the last instance'. Althusser (1969) and Poulantzas (1971) have interpreted this judicious but somewhat vague note of caution as follows. Though 'in the last instance' the economic base may determine the form of the polity, religion, the family, ideology, etc., each of these 'levels' or sectors of society also develops its own autonomous logic, proceeds at its own 'rhythm' and exerts its own influence upon the rest of society. The overall determination of these levels by the economic base means that its own contradictions will appear in displaced form within each of them; while multiple interaction between the levels means that the contradictions of each will 'over-determine'—i.e. exacerbate—those of all the others. When the contradictions contained in every level operate simultaneously to reinforce each other, then a revolutionary 'rupture' occurs.

This odd term 'over-determination', coupled with the obscure style of these writers, has evoked considerable scepticism. Is it not simply an elaborate camouflage for a 'Marxist' theory of multi-causality, identical to the conventional wisdom of sociology for the last fifty years?[1] Yet the theory retains its Marxist tint in two ways. Firstly, 'in the last instance' must mean that, if the forces and relations of production develop according to the Marxist model, the Capital–Labour contradiction constitutes in itself and in its contribution to other contradictions a *sufficient* cause of revolution. This last instance may never actually arrive, for according to Althusser the other levels will precipitate the rup-

[1] L. Kolakowski, 'Althusser's Marx', in *The Socialist Register* (1971) 119–21.

16

ture. But a process of dialectical intensification of the Capital–Labour contradiction should be occurring, and could be projected into the future. Secondly, the main contradiction experienced in each level of society must be in some way a product, though not a mere reflection, of the basic economic contradiction. It is helpful to remember Althusser's Freudian analogy of the relationship between dreams and reality: experience on one level may be displaced on to another, appearing there in a superficially quite different guise. An example given by both Althusser and Poulantzas is the religious level in late feudal society. The bourgeoisie, in first attacking religion (in, for example, the French Enlightenment), were inevitably attacking the economic structure of feudalism. Althusser has elsewhere argued that educational institutions play a role similar to religion in contemporary capitalism.[1]

There are two ways in which this general approach could be put to use. Firstly, the Capital–Labour contradiction could be assessed to see whether it could constitute 'in the last instance' a sufficient cause of a proletarian revolution. I shall do this from the point of view of the proletariat itself—is there in evidence a dialectical process of evolving class consciousness which, in the last instance, could produce a genuinely revolutionary consciousness? Obviously, the viewpoint and situation of other classes would also have to be examined if one wished to predict the likelihood of an actual and successful revolution, and this is outside the scope of my analysis here. Secondly, we can turn to the origins of other social contradictions to see to what extent, 'in the first instance', they were displaced expressions of the Capital–Labour contradiction (and to what extent a reverse process of displacement on to Capital–Labour also occurs). This would involve considerable historical scholarship and I can provide only sketchy treatment here.

Thus the theoretical disputes I have outlined devolve upon two crucial issues: (1) in mature capitalist society is the Capital–Labour conflict (which all acknowledge to exist) sufficient to generate all four elements of working-class consciousness? and

[1] 'Ideology and Ideological State Apparatuses (Notes towards an Investigation)', in *Lenin and Philosophy*, English edn (London: New Left Books, 1971).

(2) are other major social conflicts (which, again, all acknowledge) a product of the Capital–Labour conflict? I will answer
these questions by examining in the following sequence:

1. the nature of the Capital–Labour relationship in contemporary capitalism, considered statically;
2. the implications of this in terms of 'alienation' and
   'economism' for working-class consciousness, again in a
   static model;
3. the relationship of economic to non-economic conflict in the
   various countries considered;
4. a dynamic model of 'the explosion of consciousness' in conflict situations;
5. a dynamic model of the development of mature capitalist
   society based on the theory of 'the new working class'.

This is the framework for that most difficult of sociological ven-
tures, the analysis of dynamic processes.

2. INDUSTRIAL RELATIONS IN ADVANCED CAPITALISM

The values of the countries with which I am dealing remain today identifiably capitalist to the extent that they remain committed to a liberal market view of ethics and society. According to this view, freedom and justice are best secured by 'breaking down' man's needs and activities into separate segments (work, consumption, politics, etc.) and providing each one with a separate market in which individuals can express their preferences and realise their needs. It is therefore anti-totalitarian in the fullest sense, opposed to any attempt to realise total human values in a unified way. As Max Weber observed, capitalist society is relatively unethical and 'disenchanted'—the realisation of substantive, ethical aims is a byproduct of individuals and institutions pursuing their separate interests in a formally rational way, and is not actually embodied in social structure itself. What is meant by 'the end of ideology', therefore, is the acceptance by the mass of the people of this instrumental and segmented structure. Industrial or political behaviour is characterised by the separation of each sector, and implicit (though probably non-normative) acceptance of 'the laws of the market' regulating each sector. This is what I shall term the ideology of *hegemonic capitalism*.

Marxists are well aware that the segmentation of life in capitalist society constitutes an obstacle to the realisation of class consciousness. For the latter to develop, the worker must make 'connections' between his work and his family life and between his industrial and his political activity. This is assumed to be guaranteed by the centrality of work: alienation and exploitation at work will spill over into non-work spheres and unify the worker's existence. Yet at first sight the reverse might seem true today: that the worker's non-work life *compensates for* work alienation. Indeed, I shall argue that in several ways the worker's experience does not form the totality suggested by either 'end of ideology' theorists or Marxists. Several segmentations—between work and non-work, between industrial and political action, between the economic and social aspects of industrial action itself—give to class relations in contemporary capitalism their peculiarly unstable nature, their paradoxical character of unresolved and unresolvable dialectic. I shall start by examining the nature of industrial action in the West, concentrating for the moment on evidence from Britain and the United States, though, as we shall see, much of my analysis applies to all countries.

If workers possessed full class consciousness they would seek among their other goals worker control of industry and society. Such a form of control would in theory enable them to attain both material and moral fulfilment, economic sufficiency and freedom of self-expression. But very few important working-class movements have pursued this all-embracing goal with any conviction. Instead, industrial action has generally split off from political action, and industrial action itself has split into two subordinate and separate spheres: the economic and the job control spheres. By job control, I mean issues arising out of the worker's attempts to attain a measure of creativity and control within the given work process surrounding him. The type of trade-union action which corresponds to this sphere is usually termed job regulation, for it seeks to establish rules which enable the worker to exert control over the work area agreed with management to be 'his'. It is to be distinguished from economism (or instrumentalism) oriented to the pursuit of financial improvements, again within the existing structure of industry. Neither challenges the overall class structure, though both may be militant in pursuit of their goals. Furthermore, job regulation is essentially conservative—it seeks to establish *de jure* what has already occurred *de facto*, namely that workers in their relations with shop-floor management are able, informally and surreptitiously, to increase the scope of their activities by being in physical possession of the shop-floor. It is very rarely that a trade-union action is oriented toward an increase in *actual* job control, and this distinguishes

20

job regulation from instrumental demands. Why should the former be a defensive activity while the latter may be aggressive?

The principal reason for the difference is that, whereas economic rewards in the capitalist enterprise can be *collective*, job creativity–control rewards are largely *distributive*. The economic interests of rival parties can in principle be served by increasing the total reward available for share-out by collective co-operation. By contrast, there tends to be a fixed amount of work control available for distribution, and for one party to increase control the other must necessarily lose some of *its* control. It is evidently easier to obtain a working solution to conflict on the former than on the latter issue. There will usually be pressures on the rival parties, exerted by their economic exigencies, to make separate settlements of their immediate clash of economic interests independently of the general state of their confrontation. Obviously this process depends on the ability of capitalism to generate increased wealth, but in the past this has been sufficiently demonstrated to render economic compromise an acceptable alternative to prolonged confrontation.

What we call the *institutionalisation of industrial conflict* is nothing more nor less than the narrowing down of conflict to aggressive economism and defensive control. This has been taken to its furthest point by contemporary American trade unions, but it is the dominant strategy of all long-surviving unions. For, *provided the employer will play this bargaining game*, it has an inherent advantage for both parties over a wider control confrontation. If the latter were to succeed it would have to eliminate economism beforehand, for its success depends on working-class unity. Yet economism can exist in free competition with more extreme unionism, continually undercutting it by an ability to obtain interim successes from compromise bargaining. The employer will yield on economic bargaining more readily than he will on the sacred 'managerial prerogative' of control. Where economism and movements oriented to workers' control have competed, the former have usually won (Bell 1961; Taft 1964).

As trade unions are organised toward the attainment of economic bargaining gains, they tend in practice to lose sight of control issues, whether these concern the immediate work situation or wider-ranging questions of industrial structure. With the increasing trend toward productivity bargaining, job control is viewed by trade unions as something which can be exchanged periodically for economic rewards; typically workers will gain some shop-floor control informally, and indeed surreptitiously, and then formally sign it away in union–management negotiations. Where job control issues are raised positively—and there may recently have been a slight increase in the proportion of British strikes concerned with job control—this is likely to be a shop steward initiative, relatively independent of the union leadership (Cliff and Barker 1966). And wider control issues can barely be raised at all if the framework of a capitalist market is implicitly accepted by the very activity of compromise economic bargaining. This may be so even of apparently ideological unions: to anticipate my later argument, the practical relations with management entered into by Communist unions may be indistinguishable from those of reformist unions.

Unions are, of course, conflict organisations, incongruent with any extreme view of industrial harmony. Nevertheless, their economistic activities reduce the *class* nature of the conflict. This is worth stressing, for there is a tendency to view class conflict in industry as grounded in economic disputes. When we speak loosely of 'classes' in industry we normally mean manual workers on the one hand and higher management and shareholders on the other. Obviously, difficulties arise in placing intermediate groups and deciding if management and shareholders are really the same group, but these do not obscure the polarisation in real consciousness on which our distinction is based. Yet in economic terms the qualitative break is between capital and all wages and salaries, and there is no quantitative break at the 'class' divide. The break is, in fact, not financial but rather one of job control.

We can see this from the objective work situation. The manual worker is normally subjected to a very close form of managerial control. His pay is geared as closely as possible to his work effort. He is either paid by the piece he produces or by the smallest practicable unit of the time he spends working. Though most manual workers are paid by the hour, disciplinary practices generally distinguish shorter time periods; for example, three minutes late to work may lose a man fifteen minutes' pay. Where possible, management will reinforce close monetary control with the physical presence of a supervisor. From this we can deduce that the worker regards his effort as a *cost*: he exchanges effort, a cost, for wages, a benefit. Remove the close control, and he will not work. It is worth noting that this applies to virtually all manual workers, skilled as well as unskilled, and generally distinguishes them from office staff. The latter are usually assumed to have internalised the employer's work norms, while workers need coercing. Why should we doubt the almost unanimous views of Western employers on the nature of classes in industry?

Another way of testing the relative importance of economic and control issues for the development of class consciousness is to look at the situations in which the latter has developed. Evidence is available from Touraine's (1966) cross-industry study of France. Class consciousness was at its highest in industries like mining, heavy engineering and foundries, where managerial control was at its tightest, and among its lowest in the building industry, where the cash nexus relationship was comparatively clear and immediate (Chs 1-3). It has long been known, of course, that class consciousness varies directly with size of plant—the largest organisations structure work routines most rigidly, and therefore meet with most worker resistance.

Hence, to the extent that trade unions pursue economic and job control issues separately and the latter defensively, and to the extent that they do not pursue wider issues of work control, they operate to *weaken* workers' class consciousness. What are the consequences of this for the workers' own attitudes and behaviour? If we were to adopt the 'end of ideology' approach we would expect economistic and defensive control strategies to correspond to workers' own preferences. Wider creativity-control issues would have no, or negligible, salience in workers' consciousness, and workers would not be alienated.

3. WORKING-CLASS CONSCIOUSNESS – ALIENATION AND ECONOMISM

The anti-Marxist approach to these matters could actually take one of three alternative forms, and I will consider them in turn :

1. It could be conceded that men seek self realisation at work through the exercise of creativity and control, but then argued that capitalist industrial structure enables them to achieve this.
2. It could be denied that men seek such self realisation. This would contest the Marxist view of man, and raise the possibility that work conditions viewed by the Marxist as 'objectively' alienating do not produce subjective alienation.
3. The existence of work deprivation could be conceded but its importance minimised. Work deprivation might, for example, be greatly outweighed by happiness experienced outside work in capitalist society. Overall, the worker would emerge as quite content, and the Marxist would be forced to admit that the worker was not alienated. This, like the previous argument, would contest the Marxist view of man by denying the primacy of work.

The first line of attack has never been seriously sustained by a sociologist because too many facts go against it. The jobs that most workers (manual and non-manual alike) are required to perform in the contemporary West are simply not capable of extending creative powers of mastery over the material environment. Most work organisations are pyramidal in shape, and only those near the apex of the pyramid are likely to control to any significant extent their creative powers. Obsessed by large factories, the sociologists may overstate the typical amount of

24

hierarchical control exercised over the worker, but it remains nonetheless true that the work roles of most manual and lower white-collar workers are closely defined and controlled by others. For example, in current research we find that, out of over 350 different jobs across one labour market, only very few allow the worker to exercise as much intrinsic job skill as he would use if driving to work.[1] If workers did seek self realisation at work, they would not find it.

The second argument is, perhaps, more plausible, and has been made by several American industrial sociologists. It is associated with the idea that, though self realisation is not sought at all at work, it can be both sought and obtained outside of work. In this view it is only outside intellectuals, imposing their own work ethics on others, who are preoccupied by problems of work deprivation. Yet this is a false argument, as we can see from two types of evidence.

Firstly, we can look at variations in work satisfactions. The Marxist argument at this point would be that expressions of discontent with work are related to the degree to which it denies workers the exercise of creativity and control. The survey results are almost uniform in supporting the prediction. Jobs which vary objectively in terms of the opportunities they allow for creativity and control are associated in the predicted way with job satisfaction statements, satisfaction with the use of one's abilities and of freedom of expression, willingness to continue in the work and other indices of perceived deprivation.[2] Groups which do not respond in this way have been found in particular cultural milieux, but they remain an insignificant proportion of the whole.[3] Furthermore, job enlargement studies show that in

[1] Interim results of research conducted jointly with R. M. Blackburn in the Department of Applied Economics, University of Cambridge. I have excepted drivers themselves from this comparison.

[2] Blauner (1964); Kornhauser (1965); Goldthorpe *et al.* (1968); N. C. Morse and R. S. Weiss, 'The function and meaning of work and the job', *American Sociological Review* (*A.S.R.*), xx (1955).

[3] One of Blauner's groups, the Southern Textile workers, experienced much lower deprivation than the theory would have predicted, but the rest of his results, including the multi-industry

almost all cases where workers have interpreted the change as increasing their work control they have welcomed it. As a reviewer of these studies notes, such unanimity is rare in empirical sociology (Blumberg 1968). These results show that there is an underlying uniformity in Western workers' demands from work. On the basis of some of these studies, Chris Argyris (1964) has gone so far as to suggest that in contemporary society the needs of the 'mature, healthy personality' are for challenge and fulfilment in work, and that work organisations deny these needs. As a corollary, therefore, mentally defective workers probably make better employees, from the point of view of the employer (p. 67).

The second source of evidence is the objective work situation, to which I referred earlier. If workers have to be coerced to work, they must experience work deprivation—it is as simple as that. The important question is that raised by the third argument— How *salient* is this deprivation? This is a very complex issue and we must consider the empirical studies in detail.

Robert Dubin (1956) has expressed this argument in its most powerful form. In a study of American manual workers, he found that their 'central life interests' lay outside of work. He has subsequently interpreted this result as follows:

> . . . while participating in work a general attitude of apathy and indifference prevails. The response to the demands of the institutions is to satisfy the minimum expectations of required behavior without reacting affectively to these demands. Thus the industrial worker does not feel imposed upon by the tyranny of organizations, company or union. He is indifferent to this area of his life. . . . Self-realization may . . . be a matter

---

survey, support the prediction. In any case, the textile workers were probably comparing their job situation with their expectations, rather than their aspirations (see my later argument). Another special problem arises at the bottom of the job hierarchy, where the popularity of 'traction' makes workers prefer utterly undemanding jobs to those that are slightly more challenging. This is how A. N. Turner and P. R. Lawrence interpret the deviant results of their 'Town' sub-sample: *Industrial Jobs and the Worker* (Boston: Harvard University Press, 1965).

of indifference to people for whom work is not a central life interest.[1]

The Affluent Worker study in this country (Goldthorpe *et al.* 1968, 1969) has been interpreted by some as arriving at similar conclusions. W. W. Daniel, in an attack on what he sees as the implication of this study, puts it neatly when he says of the 'instrumentalism' of such workers, 'Instrumentality apparently operates like a local anaesthetic; they can see the wound but feel no pain.'[2] Like Daniel, I am sceptical of the validity of such a conclusion. There are indeed two mistakes in the argument, arising from the nature of the supporting data. I will examine these with reference to Dubin's own study.

Dubin's procedure was to question workers about the present importance of work and non-work in their lives. He presented them with fixed choice answers from which they had to choose. Examples are:

'It hurts me most if I am disliked
   —by the people at work;
   —by the people around town;
   —by anyone I know.'

and:

'When I am doing some work
   —I am usually most accurate working at home;
   —I seldom think about being accurate;
   —I am usually most accurate working at the plant.'

It is after summarising responses to such items that Dubin concludes that 76 per cent of workers had their central life interests outside of work—they largely chose the non-work alternatives. Yet there are two gaps in the argument. The first is that the

[1] *Human Relations in Administration* 2nd edn (Englewood Cliffs, New Jersey: Prentice-Hall, 1961) 79. The actual results are reported in Dubin (1956).

[2] 'Industrial Behaviour and Orientation to Work – A Critique', *Journal of Management Studies*, vi (1969). For further debate between Daniel and Goldthorpe see the May 1970 and October 1971 issues of the *Journal*.

results indicate statements of preference in the given situation, and do not necessarily reflect workers' aspirations or general views about work: they may, in fact, be mere descriptions of deprivations (Kornhauser 1965, p. 328). The second gap is that, to make his general argument, Dubin needs information about the *absolute* level of deprivation or contentment in work and non-work, and the only data he provides illuminate the *relative* levels. Thus he cannot actually tell us of the extent of workers' contentment in work and non-work, only that they are *more* content in the latter. This is by no means a denial of the Marxist argument. We have deduced that work is viewed as a cost by the workers, and we may assume that non-work is normally a benefit, but to solve the debate we need to know the exact difference between them. The problem is this: is the difference sufficient for non-work to compensate for, and reduce the salience of, work experiences?

One further point can be made on the basis of 'relative' data. Such compensation processes as do occur are not sufficient to counteract the effects of the hierarchical distribution of work rewards. In surveys, those with the most depriving jobs also felt more deprived outside of work.[1] It is highly plausible that successful instrumentalism among lower levels of work should reduce the effects of work deprivation, but the overall deprivation is still greater than among other groups. We can perceive this more clearly by looking at the exact meaning of 'satisfaction' and 'con-

[1] Kornhauser (1965) table 9.5, p. 206. For American and Italian findings see M. Kohn, *Class and Conformity* (Homewood, Illinois: The Dorsey Press, 1969); see also the negative correlation found between job satisfaction and neuroses by J. D. Handyside, 'Job Satisfaction and Aspirations', *Occupational Psychology*, xxxv (1961) and the relationship between job level and anomia in various studies, e.g. L. Srole, 'Social integration and certain corollaries: an exploratory study', *A.S.R.*, xxi (1956). For a contrary result reported for Swedish workers see M. Seeman, 'On the personal consequences of alienation in work', *A.S.R.*, xxxii (1967). Unfortunately Seeman's results are vitiated by a methodological error: by using factor analysis to isolate his variables, he prejudices the issues, for 'factors' must be necessarily unrelated to each other. The lack of correlation between work alienation and non-work deprivations may thus be due to an artefact.

tentment' with work. For satisfaction does not necessarily indicate a lack of experienced deprivation.

All we know of job satisfaction surveys indicates that workers who are satisfied with their work are comparing it, not to what they would like work to be, but to what they realistically expected it to be. Hence we find that older men are more satisfied than younger men in the same jobs. This chronological process of coming to terms with reality has been described by several authors. As Kornhauser (1965) observes '. . . men in the routine types of work come, over the years, to accept and make the most of their situation'; and 'most workers . . . accept their work life without distress and even in most cases with a kind of mild, passive, somewhat fatalistic contentment'. 'Acceptance' might seem a more appropriate term than 'contentment', as we can see if we look more closely at his findings, particularly at his index of 'mental health'. The overall index, like job satisfaction, increases with age; that is, older workers express fewer worries and anxieties. However, this conceals two different trends: with age the worker actually perceives the objective situation as being more oppressive, but he learns to adjust more easily to it (Kornhauser 1965, pp. 63–4, 77, 266). From other studies we can see that the worker develops various psychological defence mechanisms against objective reality—rationalisation, projection, daydreaming, apathy, fatalism and the like (Argyris 1964, pp. 86–95).

Kornhauser's results are crucial, for they show that the changes in attitude which occur during a man's lifetime can be attributed to the characteristics of his job: the longer his experience of depriving work, the more likely he is to come to terms with his life in a pragmatic, adjustive way. This non-normative acceptance seems to be generalised to his attitudes as a whole. The most frequent defence mechanism is fatalism. The most deprived workers develop fatalistic views about life in general: they feel their work life cannot be changed because they lack the necessary abilities, or because the bosses have always exploited the workers, or even because of the inherent selfishness of man.[1] This charac-

[1] Kornhauser (1965) 215–18; L. Lipsitz, 'Work life and political attitudes', *American Political Science Review*, LVIII (1964); and two

teristic emerges also in studies of the general lives of workers. In an earlier article (1970) I noted that radical elements of workers' consciousness in Britain and the U.S. were of the 'populist' kind—such as that 'the rich have always exploited the poor'—rather than of a class or political kind. Little sense of alternative political possibilities was present. I concluded that the compliance of the working class with the authority structure of liberal democracy rested largely on 'pragmatic acceptance' of its lowly position in society.

These results support neither the 'end of ideology' thesis nor Marxism: they reveal an extremely complex situation. The ability of any worker to generate a *total* account of his life situation is reduced by the gap that exists between work and non-work experience. Non-work clearly compensates for work alienation, at least to some extent, yet does not remove experience of the latter. Hence the worker's experience is not uniformly or even largely favourable, as the 'end of ideology' would have it. But if this is alienation it is a very passive sort, and not what Marx envisaged when he described the working class as 'abased and *indignant* at its abasement'[1] Marx's conception of alienation involved a recognition by the worker of the distance between his essential nature and potentialities and his actual existence under capitalism. Yet the data do not reveal this psychological 'distancing'. Kornhauser's findings and Argyris's commentary are especially relevant here. The former shows how the worker progressively comes to terms with reality by steadily lowering his aspiration. By middle age the gap has disappeared and he may even seem 'content'. Argyris describes how the worker gradually internalises the demands of the organisation and resolves the initial discrepancy in individual psychological terms with guilt feelings or lowered psychological investment in work. Even the worker's fatalistic attitudes do not express a sense of distance, for the gap between desire and actuality is considered unbridgeable.

articles by J. E. Horton and W. E. Thompson, 'Powerlessness and political negativism', *A.J.S.*, LXVII (1962) and 'Political alienation as a force in political action', *Social Forces*, XXXVIII (1960).

[1] *The Holy Family*; in L. D. Easton and K. H. Guddat, *Writings of the Young Marx on Philosophy and Society* (Garden City, New York: Doubleday–Anchor Books, 1967) 367.

The ability to transcend such a state of consciousness seems absent —the conception of an *alternative* is lacking.

Furthermore, the results show that the conception of alternative is most absent where workers' experience is most *total*, that is among the unskilled workers whose passive alienation spills over into their whole life. The most alienated workers are not the most revolutionary, for the necessary confidence in their own *power* is lacking.

There is, however, another sense in which the worker's experience of reality could be viewed as a total one, and this view is increasingly popular among contemporary neo-Marxists. The gap between work and non-work can be recognised, but both can be seen as subservient to the rampant commercialism of the contemporary West. Andre Gorz (1965) has described this process:

> . . . The further it goes . . . the more it numbs a stunted mass-produced humanity with satisfactions that leave the basic dissatisfaction untouched, but still distract the mind from it: the more it hopes that these men, preoccupied with various means of escape and oblivion, will forget to question the basis of the whole system: the alienation of labour. (p. 349)

This polemic carries its own pitfalls. If passivity is so all-embracing, how can the worker overcome alienation? Many radicals realise the force of this argument, and hence Marcuse and others have abandoned their hopes in the revolutionary proletariat. Marcuse sees passive acceptance as even leading to the kind of 'satisfaction' with capitalism that I have already described, and, as he recognises, this makes the very notion of alienation questionable. He argues that this

> . . . constitutes a more progressive stage of alienation. The latter has become entirely objective; the subject which is alienated is swallowed up by its alienated existence. There is only one dimension, and it is everywhere and in all forms.[1]

[1] H. Marcuse, *One Dimensional Man* (London: Sphere Books paperback edn, 1968) 24–6.

This is not dialectical materialism, for the worker's experience of material contradictions is apparently insufficient to transcend his 'false consciousness'. Gorz has realised this in the second (1969) edition of his book. Reacting possibly against his earlier argument, and explicitly attacking Marcuse, he states:

> The critique of the capitalist system that we outline is based neither on an *a priori* view of 'human nature' nor on idealism. It is based on the reality of an historical *praxis* by which man reveals and makes himself capable of control in the very activities of social production . . . human *praxis* has a specific reality which is neither the same as its objectified consequences nor exhausted in them: in alienation, it encounters them as its own negation. (p. 16)

Or, in less Hegelian language, alienation is recognised and transcended by working-class consciousness and action.

Is it in fact, however? The main difficulty confronting this kind of argument is that, whereas one can observe working-class protest movements in all countries directed against industrial exploitation, protest is notably lacking in the sphere of consumption except among exclusively middle-class groups. Even during May–June 1968 in France, when (as we shall see) a variety of new kinds of protest emerged, complaints about the 'all-round commercialisation' of the quality of life were heard from middle-class intellectuals, not from workers. Indeed, working-class socialists will reject these complaints—for them an adequate level of material consumption is not guaranteed even in contemporary society. For the worker there is a real gap between the quality of work and non-work life, one that acts as a barrier against the totality of class consciousness.

It is now evident that the almost exclusive preoccupation of trade unions with economism is not a mere case of 'betrayal' by their leadership: it is rooted in the worker's very experience, and he reinforces the union's position. Normally confronted by an employer who will budge on economic but not on control issues, the worker takes what he can easily get and attempts to reduce the salience of what is denied him. Though this leaves him partially alienated, it does not place him, as it were, 'outside' the

32

structure of capitalist society, but rather compromised by it.
Hence he grasps neither the totality of society nor alternative
structures.

Such processes are evident in all Western countries, for they
are inherent in the nature of the worker's contract of employment
in capitalism. Forced to alienate his own productive powers in
return for economic rewards, the worker develops a *dualistic
consciousness*, in which control and money, work and non-work,
become separated. However, this has different effects upon
different labour movements, as we can see by turning to a comparative perspective.

4. INTERNATIONAL VARIATIONS IN CONSCIOUSNESS

In France and Italy working-class organisations stand out in marked contrast to those of most other Western countries. Their largest working-class parties and trade-union federations (the C.G.T. in France, the C.G.I.L. in Italy) are Communist-led and are apparently dedicated to revolutionary ends, being resolutely opposed to reform from within capitalism. When we look closely at their conference resolutions and their propaganda, we find virulent anti-capitalism, elaborate programmes for nationalisation and centralised yet democratic planning and a close analysis of the 'Workers' Fatherland', the Soviet Union. All this is bound together in metaphors of continual class struggle. The contrast with British and American industrial and political leaders is striking—the British will go so far as to talk about 'the working class', Americans only risk 'the working man'. Neither discusses alternative societies. However, there is one notable hiatus in the French and Italian vision, namely a programme for the revolution itself. The method by which the workers are to reach socialism is left relatively vague, especially in France. There is consequently a flavour of unreality, of utopianism even, about the Communist movement's aims. This has also been transmitted to the rival socialist parties and union federations, which tend to put forward competing views of an entire, though not always coherent, alternative society. This has been especially true of the Italian Socialist Party and of the second largest French union federation, the C.F.D.T., which in the 1960s flirted with 'democratic planning' and 'self-management'.[1]

[1] The official *Histoire du Parti Communiste Français* (Paris: Éditions Sociales, 1964); D. L. Horowitz (1963) 238, 334–6; T. H. Greene, 'The Communist Parties of Italy and France', *World Politics*, XXI

In general terms, therefore, union and party militants tend to have a revolutionary view of society—capitalism cannot be reformed, for it is 'inefficient, irrational and immoral'.[1] These views then penetrate the shop floor. Various pieces of survey evidence indicate that the ideologies of most British and American workers stand in marked contrast to those of most French and Italian workers. A rare piece of truly comparative evidence is provided by the 'football team' analogy, in which workers are asked whether employers and workers are on the same side or on different sides. The majority of British workers reply 'the same side'. This has been replicated in three studies: 67 per cent of the Luton 'affluent workers', 70 per cent of process workers in various regions and in two studies, and 80 per cent of Banbury factory workers reply thus.[2] By contrast, in a French study of iron and steel workers, only 28 per cent thought they were on the same side, a finding reinforced in this and in another French study by the large majority of workers who said also that the interests of employers and workers were opposed.[3] These differences are marked. Hamilton's (1967) presentation or survey data from France and Italy enable us to explain them (pp. 56–7). Workers in both countries were asked to arrange a list of countries in the order in which they thought the workers were happiest. Seven countries were presented, including the Soviet Union and the United States. Among French workers, 14 per cent ranked the Soviet Union first and 11 per cent second; among the Italians, 19 per cent ranked the Soviet Union first and 13 per cent second. Those French workers who placed the Soviet

---

(1968); A.-J. Stern et al. 'Factions and Opinion Groups in European Mass Parties', Comparative Politics, III (1971).

[1] See C. A. Micaud's very unsympathetic account of interviews with Communist worker militants, Communism and the French Left (London: Weidenfeld & Nicolson, 1963) 104–16.

[2] Goldthorpe et al. (1968) 73; S. Cotgrove and C. Vamplew, 'Technology, Class and Politics: the Case of Process Workers', Sociology, VI (1972); D. Wedderburn and R. Crompton, Workers' Attitudes and Technology (Cambridge University Press, 1972).

[3] Willener (1967) 92–3; O. Benoit, 'Statut dans l'enterprise et attitudes syndicales des ouvriers', Sociologie du Travail, IV (1962); cf. also Touraine (1966) 171.

Union first also placed the United States last (this datum is not reported for the Italians). The influence of Communism is shown by the predominance of C.G.T. and C.G.I.L. members among the pro-Soviet group. The favourable comments made on the Soviet Union also reflect Communist propaganda: it was thought to offer extensive welfare arrangements, 'workers' government', socialism, 'working for an ideal' and the absence of exploitation. As many as a quarter of French workers believed that their party should take power by non-constitutional means and saw improvement as coming only from revolution. They were also disproportionately C.G.T. and pro-Soviet. This cluster of attitudes reveals that a large minority of French workers possesses the basic elements of the Soviet version of socialist ideology. Almost certainly this finds little reflection in either Britain or the United States, though there is no directly comparable evidence available. I have noted elsewhere (1970) that, in terms of the political and industrial *action* they advocate, British and American workers are surprisingly conservative. This is also a conclusion of *The Affluent Worker* study, in which 69 per cent of the sample believed that class inequalities were *necessary* features of society (and nearly all the remainder gave incoherent answers) (Goldthorpe *et al.* 1969, p. 154). It seems apparent that workers in some cultural settings are aware of alternative ideologies and in others are not. This has consequences for job satisfaction. If we consider reformist unions, satisfaction varies positively with union membership and activism; that is, the most satisfied workers are union activists, followed by non-active members. This is true for unions in the United States and also for the moderate *Force Ouvrière* in France. But the reverse is true for the Communist C.G.T. in France, in which the activists are the most dissatisfied.[1] The possession of an *alternative* ideology seems to be associated here with dissatisfaction with one's present situation, the lack of it with a passive, 'satisfied' acceptance of deprivation.

[1] For the U.S. see W. Spinrad, 'Correlates of trade union participation: a summary of the literature', *A.S.R.*, xxv (1960); for France see Hamilton (1967) 239–41: with the third French federation, the then Catholic C.F.T.C. (now the C.F.D.T.), there is no relationship either way.

Thus union tactics are in a sense circular. Reformist unions tacitly abandon wider issues of worker control. They fail to articulate the experience of work deprivation and are often prepared to sign away job control rights in return for wage concessions.[1] But in doing this they help close off alternatives to the worker, and thereby reconcile him more easily to his deprivation. Conversely, revolutionary unions might be said to foster job dissatisfaction which then reinforces their demands for worker control. It is, however, dangerous to emphasise the autonomy of the union leadership in making its choice. I do not wish to argue either that reformist leaders have sold out, or that revolutionaries mislead their followers. There are many cases in which the opposite seems true. In Britain, for example, the reformist leadership of the mining and iron and steel unions was consistently in advance of its membership in pressing for public ownership and for some measure of workers' control (Banks 1970). And the reverse trend, revolutionary leadership indulging in reformist action, is even more frequent.

We cannot fail to be impressed by the ideology of the Communist parties and unions, for they parade it publicly. How far it affects their actions, however, is an open question. Regardless of their ultimate objectives, they are implicated in the day-to-day bargaining processes which keep greased the wheels of capitalism. The union militant and official is therefore in a highly ambiguous situation, one where there is a lack of fit between his ideology and his action. This helps to account for the utopian quality of the ideology, which I noted earlier. It is heightened by the belief, normal among both reformist and revolutionary officials, that they are more militant than the ordinary worker. Hence, in Italy the three union federations differ more in beliefs than actions, while in France a recent study of union militants found no direct correlation between their class ideologies and the type of trade-union action they advocated (Raffaele 1962 Ch. 4; Vidal 1968). Even in these countries, therefore, strong pressures are exercised upon working-class leaders by the short-term economic interdependence of employers and workers. The continuous dialectic

[1] Though it must be conceded that they show more of an interest in the narrower aspects of job control than do revolutionary unions, probably because they guarantee a certain bargaining strength.

between this pressure and class consciousness gives to industrial relations in France and Italy their unstable character, which I will explore later on. If consciousness is dualistic, so too are actions.

In these countries, therefore, workers' consciousness assumes an even more complex character than in 'reformist' countries like Britain and the United States. As yet, no simple answer can be given to the question, 'Is the working class a revolutionary force?' Before we can attempt this, two other questions must be discussed. Why is class consciousness higher in France and Italy? and What happens when compromised labour leaders lose control of their members?

5. CAPITALIST HEGEMONY

In this section I wish to present, somewhat tentatively, a modified version of the 'end of ideology' theory. I will argue that, where capitalism becomes hegemonic and eliminates 'archaic' institutions, the *diversity* of forms of organised consciousness declines among *both* the working and the employing class, leaving both groups dominated by moderate, segmented, reformist ideologies. This is not an inevitable process, but it depends critically on non-capitalist elements of society. Where it has not yet occurred there are no good reasons to suppose that it will occur in the future.

We must remember that a truly capitalist ideology is opposed not only to that of socialism but also to that of the earlier 'feudal' period. Simplifying somewhat, feudalism emphasised the *diffuseness* of the ties of rights and duties binding together social classes : landlord and tenant are bound by social, economic, religious and moral ties and not—like the capitalist and worker—by a narrow cash nexus. In feudal society, when these ties break down the injured party couches its protest in moral and religious terms. Neither conservative nor radical views within feudalism are receptive to the notion that social relations might be governed by the mechanisms of the economic market. Opposition to these mechanisms is thus found in the early stages of industrialisation, and also in countries characterised by uneven development.

First, I will consider such opposition with respect to workers' consciousness. The conventional sociological view of the 'feudal' and 'deferential' worker located him principally in rural situations or in towns which are assumed to be dominated by rural, pre-industrial values. Indeed, there is much evidence to support

39

this view.[1] But at the same time, there is increasing evidence from a variety of countries to show that extreme *left* movements may also derive much support from these locations. In Finland, Allardt has shown that one of the two main sources of Communist Party support is among workers in newly-industrialised rural areas.[2] In the United States, Leggett (1968) has found more class consciousness among workers from agrarian than industrial backgrounds. Reviewing French studies, Hamilton (1967, Ch. 11) finds unusual support for Communist attitudes among workers migrating from the rural south and centre of France. In all these cases 'uprootedness' (Leggett's term) is evident: either the workers have migrated from rural to urban areas, or the rural area is itself in the process of transformation. Leftist attitudes do not, however, seem a necessary consequence of uprootedness (as Leggett suggests): for example, Linz[3] has found disproportionately *conservative* attitudes in Germany among workers who have migrated from rural areas. It seems safer to endorse Hamilton's view that these men have unusually volatile attitudes. In the case of his own French workers, they bring in a 'pre-radical' disposition, which contact with organised Communism can swiftly transform into class consciousness and revolutionary ardour. As Hamilton notes, the direction of the shift may reflect their pre-industrial experience. Where the worker has previously lived in a share-cropping area where both Church and landlord are virtually absent, pre-radicalism will be evident, as among the workers from the French Midi; where he has lived under the close control of landlord and Church, as in the German case, he will be extremely conservative and deferential.

To these rural influences we must add pre-industrial political influences. Where class polarisation existed prior to the industrial revolution, this carried over to the capitalist era. As Lichtheim

[1] D. Lockwood, 'Sources of variation in working class images of society', *Sociological Review*, xiv (1966).

[2] E. Allardt, 'Types of Protest and Alienation', in Allardt and S. Rokkan, *Mass Politics* (New York: The Free Press, 1970).

[3] Juan Linz, unpublished thesis referred to by Hamilton (1967) 258. Allardt also notes that migrants to the major industrial areas of Finland tend to be social Democrats rather than Communists.

notes,[1] Communism and class polarisation in France owe much to the revolutionary Jacobin tradition, while in Italy present-day industrial extremism is traceable directly to the 'revoltist tradition' of rural Italian society which has acted as a barrier against the incorporation of working-class leadership into the Italian establishment. Conversely, the compromise politics of industrial Britain can take place because class conflict was managed over a century before industrialisation (Moore 1969).

Two conclusions stand out from this. Firstly, the diversity of pre-industrial settings gave rise in the industrialising countries to a great diversity of ideological responses among workers. Secondly, some settings encouraged the emergence of revolutionary sentiments among the working class. Moreover, there is evidence to suggest that these sentiments take on a socialist character at *the initial point of contact with large-scale industrial production*. Touraine's (1966) cross-sectional study of industries in contemporary France provides this evidence. As I noted before, the most class-conscious and revolutionary workers were those with an existing sense of occupational identity who were now being threatened by the tight job-control system of mass production: miners, foundry workers, skilled engineering workers. As he observes: 'Class consciousness is consciousness of the drama lived out by the worker at the moment he encounters rationalisation and industrial organisation' (p. 341); for most workers, this 'moment' seems to have been located at an early stage of industrialisation.

Such processes are reinforced by the ideologies of ruling classes themselves. In the early years of industrialisation many employers found it difficult to accept as legitimate the capitalist mode of social control, the cash nexus. Instead, their views on their property rights were considerably more diffuse, involving ownership rights over the workers and the workers' families. Only gradually did their claims narrow and their employers content themselves with a bureaucratic, economically-based mode of control over their work-force.[2] Even today, diffuse paternalism is

[1] G. Lichtheim, *Marxism in Modern France* (New York: Columbia University Press, 1966); Horowitz (1963) 326-7.

[2] R. Bendix, *Work and Authority in Industry* (New York: Harper and Row, 1963).

evident in almost all managerial ideologies, though usually in its watered-down, 'happy family' version, more an appeal for fellowship than a demand for obedience. Where it survives in stronger form it is often associated with particular *religious* commitment—Quaker in the Anglo-Saxon world, Catholic in the Latin world. As such it has been traditionally hostile to trade unionism, which is seen as bringing 'outside' influences into the 'family' : workers are 'misled', and employers are forced to act in the workers' own interests by opposing the unions. Among some French employers these views are so strongly held that they amount to feudal property demands (Willener 1967). The refusal of French and Italian employers to co-operate with trade unions in 'their' factories has always been observed to be a very potent encouragement to Communism among the workers. The intransigence of employers has often been reinforced by political ruling groups; in France and Italy, their lukewarm support for democracy and their flirtations with fascism, as well as their unwillingness to compromise with working-class movements, has been noted as a divisive factor in society at large (Gorz 1969, Ch. 1; Touraine 1968; Lipset 1964; Ross and Hartmann 1960).

From these findings it seems evident that the more employers behave as true capitalists, the securer will they rest in their beds! It is in those countries where employers have been least willing and able to act within the narrowly capitalist frame of reference that the working class has come closest to achieving revolution (tsarist Russia, Wilhelmian Germany, contemporary France and Italy). It is also in the most capitalist countries (Britain and the United States) that the working class has become most reformist.

In the development of industrial relations the initiative, and most of the power, lies with the employer and the government. If they take the path of compromise and adopt the language of market bargaining, then working-class economistic and reformist tendencies are greatly strengthened. It is the growth of capitalist hegemony that has produced a decline in socialist ideology in certain countries. What has actually disappeared from these countries is the *diversity* of action orientations among labour movements, for a decline in extremely conservative views could be equally documented.[1] This is not, however, an *inevitable* process of decline. There are more ways of organising an industrial society than either Marxists or functionalists would have us believe. The failure in France and Italy of a purely capitalist ideology to achieve a hegemonic position does not mean that their 'archaic' feudal elements must disappear, even if they are 'inefficient'. There is as yet no sign of the 'modernisation' so yearned for by French and Italian liberals.

I have located major determinants of contemporary class consciousness outside the necessary structure of capitalism itself. Are they also outside the economic sector of society, or can they be fitted into a Marxist theory of uneven development? Answering this would involve raising the whole Marx–Weber controversy over the link between religion and economic action, as well as assessing the nature of such phenomena as the French Revolution, the Risorgimento and Fascism. And what weight should we give to the impact of 'external' factors, like the occupation of France and the consequent collaboration with, and resistance to, the Nazis? It is worth noting that Barrington Moore (1969) has given a materialist interpretation of the differences between English and French development in terms of the economic sector in the two countries, but he has been criticised for neglecting religious, philosophical and scientific influences.[2] The problem is immense and I cannot provide an answer here.

Yet already a curiosity has emerged. It is one thing to assert that revolutions *can* occur in situations of uneven development; it is quite another to show that they occur *only* then. If working-class consciousness varies inversely with the degree of capitalist maturity in a whole society, what are we to make of orthodox Marxism? I will return to this question later.

My analysis of working-class consciousness has so far been largely static. And this is to miss an essential point of Marxist theory—that consciousness is a developing phenomenon, a process not of being but of becoming. There are still two ways in which this might be demonstrated. The first of these is through

[1] e.g. the decline of deferential voting among the English working class: R. T. McKenzie and A. Silver, *Angels in Marble* (London: Heinemann, 1968).

[2] D. Lowenthal in a review article in *History and Theory*, VII (1968).

43

'the explosion of consciousness', in which reformism is overtaken by a sudden expansion in alienation and in consciousness. The second is to point to a more recent long-term change within capitalism, and to assert that a 'new working class' is now being created which will be more class-conscious and revolutionary than the old one. I will consider these in turn.

6. THE EXPLOSION OF CONSCIOUSNESS

The starting-point for the thesis of the explosion of consciousness is a quotation from Marx which has become one of the favourites of twentieth-century Marxists:

> It is not a question of what this or that proletarian or even the whole proletariat momentarily *imagines* to be the aim. It is a question of what the proletariat *is* and what it *consequently* is historically compelled to do.[1]

This has led to a dual conception of consciousness among Marxists from Lukacs onwards: on the one hand, *actual* consciousness (what the worker normally thinks); on the other, *possible* consciousness (what Marxists know will or can occur).[2] This dualism is often expressed in a very idealist way, with the writer merely asserting an 'objective' knowledge of the laws of history which is supra-empirical. Such a position is beyond argument—either one has faith or one has not. Yet it can take a more materialist form, in which possible consciousness normally exists in a latent form and 'explodes' into action during specified revolutionary situations. The transition is thought to occur swiftly and with little prior warning. The 'old-fashioned' view of class consciousness, which sees it as a steady step-by-step progression, is dismissed. Great importance is attached to the unruly strike as the locus of the explosion, and the events of May 1968 in France

---

[1] *The Holy Family*, 368.
[2] e.g. L. Goldmann, 'Conscience Réelle et Conscience Possible...', *Transactions of the Fourth World Congress of Sociology* (1959); G. Lukacs, *History and Class Consciousness*, London edn (London: Merlin Books, 1971) 51.

are seen as its paradigm case in recent years. The need is now for 'a theory of dual consciousness'.[1]

As yet, however, this theory has not been forthcoming, and 'the explosion of consciousness' seems a rather mysterious, and in some ways metaphysical, process. Marxists over-emphasise the split between the two forms of consciousness, and hence the only way that one theory can join the two is with an emphasis on the 'myth' and the violence of strikes, which would have greatly pleased Sorel but horrified Marx. This over-emphasis often results from a desire to attack 'bourgeois' empirical sociology, with its supposed stress on actual consciousness. Robin Blackburn (1967), for example, developed his version of the explosion of consciousness in an attack upon the findings of *The Affluent Worker* sub-sample of Vauxhall car-workers. He claims that the survey, thorough as it was, could not predict the explosion of a subsequent strike because surveys must necessarily reflect mere actual consciousness. If he had read the study thoroughly, however, he would have noticed that the survey *does* reflect dynamic tensions of dual consciousness. Though the workers surveyed had mainly harmonistic views of industry, they were *also* conscious of elements of 'coercion and exploitation' in their employment relationship. If these came to the fore, more conflictual industrial relations could develop. In fact, from surveys we can easily perceive 'latent' consciousness of class, which, in certain situations, can explode. Hence it is not difficult to develop a theory of dual consciousness, and I shall do this below.

A Marxist theory of the explosion of consciousness would run as follows. In 'normal' situations the worker experiences his work as an alien force acting upon him. Though at this stage he is not class-conscious, and may adhere to a conservative ideology, he nevertheless dislikes his situation and seeks ways to avoid it. His compliance is 'pragmatic' and must be explained by an analysis of the balance of power in industry. If this balance is disturbed, as for example in some strike situations, his rejection of his situation will become perfectly evident. It is at this stage that he begins to expand his consciousness. The power of the emergent

---

[1] 'Editorial', *New Left Review* (1968), No. 52 (see also the articles by Mandel, Glucksmann and Gorz in the same issue); H. Lefèbvre, *The Explosion* (New York: Monthly Review Press, 1970).

working class is a collective power, and it is through the experience of solidarity with other workers that a worker experiences in a very concrete way the power that will eventually lead to the collective control by the workers of the means of production. Collective action will normally 'fail', or appear to achieve only limited ends, but its real significance lies in the growth of class consciousness through everyday experiences. Hence two processes occur simultaneously: a steady learning process by the workers, and short-term cycles of conflict emergence and resolution. As the former of these continues, the disjunction between the workers' apparent consciousnesses in normal situations and strike situations will grow wider. While one remains passive, being a realistic appraisal of the balance of power in that period, the other grows more socialistic as the workers learn to make the connection between their own collective action and alternative possible ways of organising production. 'Explosiveness' will thus increase until it triggers off the proletarian revolution.

Of course, we must cavil at the inevitability of this process, and should add two riders to the argument. Firstly, it appears to give too much emphasis to purely industrial conflict. Once the process is under way, it must become also political if it is to achieve a revolution. The word 'strike' has attained a rather limited meaning in English, and if we read, for example, Rosa Luxemburg's classic analysis of the 1905 strike in Russia,[1] we must remember that she is describing another explosive process: the translation of specific industrial demands into general, political demands. Secondly, the above argument over-emphasises the steadiness of the growth in latent class consciousness, suggesting that a cumulative process has been under way since the very first strike under capitalism. This would be highly misleading. Many contrary processes are at work, and particularly heavy defeats or, indeed, economistic gains in strikes may set back a development in consciousness. Nevertheless, it must be observed that the 'explosion' theory does depend on some such cumulative process, whether this be short- or long-term.

I would like to emphasise one particular aspect of this theory. Marxists predict not only that there will be a proletarian revolu-

[1] *The Mass Strike* (London, Merlin Press).

47

tion, but also that this revolution will replace capitalism with a specified alternative system, socialism. This new society conditions the form of the revolution itself: collective experiences herald the new collective organisation of production. Hence 'explosions' must be in the direction of collectivism, firstly in the form of sentiments of solidarity with other workers, and secondly in the grasping by workers of an *alternative* socialist ideology. Both must be present for a proletarian revolution to take place. We will see below that the division between the two acts as a crucial watershed in contemporary class consciousness.

There is at least surface plausibility to the 'explosion' thesis. It has often been observed that management–worker conflicts which appear to be conducted in rather confused terms bring to the surface generalised worker discontents which had hitherto escaped notice. This is most evident when the company concerned had previously been stable and paternalist, for in such cases the workers appear to have switched suddenly from deference to class consciousness. However institutionalised industrial relations become, strikes reveal the workers' pent-up feelings, deprivations and hostility to the employer.

One such incident in Britain has been well-documented. This is the 1966 strike at Vauxhall Motors, Luton, Bedfordshire. Only months before the strike, Vauxhall workers had been interviewed in *The Affluent Worker* research project, and 79 per cent of them had chosen the 'same side' answer to the football team analogy of industrial relations. During the strike, however, 'near riot conditions developed. . . . Two thousand workers . . . tried to storm the main offices. Dozens of police were brought in. . . . "The Red Flag" was sung, and workers shouted that the directors should be "strung up" ' (quoted by Blackburn 1967).

Dramatic as this appears, however, did it leave any aftermath? The strike subsided days later when specific grievances were settled. Subsequent industrial relations in the firm have been normal, with long periods of calm interspersed with small-scale and short-lived strikes. Where is the evidence for its *cumulative* effect? In fact, there are three great limitations placed upon this kind of explosive strike in the British context.

Firstly, the intentions of the workers must be regarded with some scepticism. How can 'dozens' of policemen hold back

48

'thousands' of workers? In France or Italy para-military riot police would be needed. Is it not more plausible that this was a *demonstration* to impress management and union negotiators of the seriousness of their grievances? It is always a possibility that such a demonstration will get out of hand, but the workers' representatives will attempt to restrain it; for they view the turbulence *tactically*, as convincing management that they are desperately holding back the workers from excessive violence. Once management has given in to their specific bargaining demands they will see no further point to the agitation.

Secondly, the bargaining mentality is reinforced by the de-centralised structure of negotiations. Employer and shop-floor representatives meet face-to-face in the processing of most British (and American) strikes. Representatives are thus closer to their members than they are in France or Italy, and thus 'exploding consciousness' interacts sooner with, and is more easily restrained by, union bargaining tactics. In Italy, by contrast, one commentator has noticed how the complete absence of regular channels of communication between individual employers and unions leads to strikes taking on an 'insurrectionist and emotional character'. It is not possible to use the workers' attitudes as a 'means of building up in systematic fashion an increasing ground-swell of pressure' toward negotiation and settlement (Raffaele 1962, pp. 283–5, 288–95).

The third limitation is the most fundamental, for it casts doubt upon the nature of the 'explosion' itself. It may be doubted whether there is indeed a systematic shift leftward during British strikes. This is certainly the implication of one close-quarters study of a strike in a Scottish coal mine. The authors were also impressed by the turbulence and the spontaneity of the events. 'Crowd scenes' and shouting matches were normal. However, alongside radical slogans were heard conservative ones: 'It's wrong to strike' competed with 'The only thing they understand is a strike'. Both sets of slogans struck immediate chords of response in most workers, and their overall attitudes continually oscillated.[1]

Even if we concede that the normal shift during strikes is left-

[1] T. T. Paterson and F. J. Willett, 'Unofficial strike', *Sociological Review*, XLIII (1951).

ward, we must observe that it is only *certain* leftist slogans that emerge. Hiller (1928), in his classic analysis of strikes in Britain and the U.S., noted the upsurge in sentiments such as 'the rights of labor', 'brotherhood', and 'solidarity'. These emergent sentiments of collective *identity* are, of course, in line with Marx's own theory, and we find remarkable support for Marx in the clash which occurs during strikes between the emergent collectivism of the workers and the pre-existing individualist values of bourgeois society. It has long been a puzzle to 'economic' theorists of social behaviour why organisations like trade unions can command mass membership; for, if the individual worker calculates his own costs and benefits, the cost of membership (in money, time and employer punishment) will normally outweigh the benefits. During the normal wage claim strike, when the employer has made an offer but seen it rejected, the cost of continuing the strike may often seem too high to the *individual* worker. Yet the sum of individual preferences may not be the only definition of the collective good. This is at the back of unions' characteristic rejection of secret ballots (for mass meetings) during strikes. Employers and mass media normally regard this as intimidation of the silent majority by the militants, but this is too simple (and biased) an explanation, as we can see from the recent study of the Pilkington strike (Lane and Roberts 1971). When they conducted a survey during the strike the authors found that a majority of strikers were in favour of abandoning the strike. Yet this majority actually believed itself to be a minority, and almost all its members were unwilling to incur moral disapproval (and possibly physical violence) from the supposed majority by openly advocating a return to work. And, in fact, the strike was 100 per cent solid, despite majority opinion and the opposition of the official trade union. The workers' spontaneous source of *identity* is collective solidarity with each other: each responds almost automatically to what he perceives as being the group's goals, even if he believes them to be irrational.

Thus strikes are not purely instrumental. During a strike a new form of rationality emerges, one based not on a summation of individual calculations but on collectivism *as an end in itself*. This, however, is its very weakness. For according to Marx there should be two aspects of emergent collectivism: sentiments of

50

solidarity, and socialism. The former should be instrumental to the achievement of the latter. But in Britain, emergent consciousness stops short at the former. As no alternative society is conceived as possible, solidarity cannot be instrumental to long-term ends.

The 'explosion of consciousness' in Britain has two main aspects, therefore. One is its *tactical* use—it helps persuade employers to grant concessions and helps to 'win' strikes (in a short-term sense). The other seems entirely without material use : it is the expansion of a consciousness which is 'free-floating', which does not affect action and which must necessarily subside again. In this setting, 'explosion' is an apt metaphor—it bangs but it cannot build. To see examples of explosions with greater material consequences, we must turn to other countries.

Belgium offers an interesting midway case between Britain and France in the characteristics of its industrial relations, and we have good data available on its most celebrated 'explosion' in recent years, the general strike of 1960–1. This was a violent and turbulent strike, which broke out of purely industrial bounds and involved factory occupation and street barricades. The unions, uneasily poised between revolutionary and reformist stances, were swiftly overtaken by shop-floor militants. Workers interviewed just before the strike were also 'midway' in their ideologies : they were extremely conscious of class conflict in industry but fatalistic about chances of change. They were apathetic trade unionists, hostile to political strikes and completely ignorant of radical reform programmes. But months later, the author of a study of these events was surprised to see these very workers leading the general strike. He concludes :

> The experience of these strikers in the heat of the action, in a climate of social strife, brought forward profound changes in working-class consciousness : political and ideological growth, the spread of a programme of structural reform, active trade union participation, the grasping of sentiments of class solidarity and of the necessity of collective action. . . .[1]

[1] M. Bolle de Bal, 'Les sociologues, la conscience de classe et la grande grève belge de l'hiver 60–61', *Revue de l'Institut de Sociologie*, no. 3 (1961). Quotation from pp. 577–8 (my translation).

Yet such a change did not materialise out of 'thin air'. Another writer notes that the strikers were most active in areas which the trade unions had organised most thoroughly; their consciousness could only have been acquired through the union. He argues: '. . . the explosion is due to the discrepancy perceived by the workers between the ideological themes disseminated by the trade union organisation and the latter's own actions.'[1] In this situation the role of the unions was contradictory—promoters of a consciousness which then attacks its own 'betrayal'.

In the even more dramatic events of May–June 1968, in France, the unions and the Communist Party played the same contradictory role. Though many newcomers were brought into working-class politics by the events, the key initiating role in most plants was played by the union militants. In one sample of 182 factories in the north of France, 73 per cent of the work-forces followed the call of the union militants, and in only 15 per cent of cases was the strike originated wholly independently of the militants. In another sample, of 45 firms, the role of militants was insignificant in only 8 cases. Even where the workers set up novel forms of strike action, bypassing the union hierarchy, this was more likely to be in factories that were already highly organised by the C.G.T. (Dubois *et al.* 1971, pp. 273, 345, 392). And yet, as all reports indicate, the C.G.T., the parties of the Left including the Communist Party and (to a lesser extent) the C.F.D.T. did not accept the revolutionary reality of the movement, but accepted the Grenelle compromise and eventually betrayed their own militants.

This contradictory role of the organisations creates an unstable yet possibly insoluble situation. This is dialectic without a synthesis: revolutionary consciousness and compromising institutions, each largely ignoring the presence of the other. Some Marxists see the problem only too clearly. Gorz (1969), for example, reflects sombrely that with archaic France absolutely ripe for revolution, the Left has so far failed to steer between the exciting but ineffectual spontaneity of the masses and the efficient organisation but gross hypocrisy of the Communist Party (Ch.

[1] M. Chaumont, 'Grèves, syndicalisme et attitudes ouvrières: les grèves belges de decembre 1960–janvier 1961', *Sociologie du Travail*, IV (1962) 156.

1). Yet the events of May–June 1968 were not as merely circular as those of the previous strikes I described. Ritual there certainly was, both in the class confrontation of employers and workers and in the compromises they eventually adopted. However, new developments occurred which certainly strengthened the revolutionary prospects of the French proletariat. In the first place, the mass strike itself brought results, not just in terms of material rewards but also in trade-union and worker control in matters of job regulation. The study by Dubois *et al.* (1971) showed that most militants were pleased with these gains, and hopeful that the strike had politically educated the workers to try again in the future.

Secondly, the May events produced an upsurge in worker interest in the construction of an *alternative* society. I have already noted that the programmes of the working-class organisations contained a crucial area of vagueness where their revolutionary programmes were supposed to be. When, therefore, workers began perceiving the extreme implications of their actions, they received little guidance from their traditional leadership. Unhindered by the responsibilities of compromise politics, their actions were often radical and innovative. This can be seen in the study by Dubois and his colleagues. In their sample 47 per cent of the factories affected by the strike were occupied, itself a relatively unusual event. Furthermore, in 76 per cent of cases the workers formed 'General Assemblies' in which they met in large numbers to discuss both specific and general demands. The Assemblies were part of the democratisation of the movement, being subversive of the normal hierarchical system of worker representation (though most were dominated by the trade-union activists). Their discussions were wide-ranging, and in 25 per cent of cases concerned workers' control—this became the main goal of the occupation in 19 per cent of the cases. Thus a minority of workers were discussing very concrete aspects of an alternative industrial structure. This was not narrowly conceived, and in 40 per cent of the cases discussions with *cadres* (lower and middle management) were entered into. All of these initiatives, together with the ideals of 'workers' power' and *auto-gestion*, eventually foundered and were seen to be utopian in the France of June–July 1968. Yet they were the first sign of major dialectical progress in the French working-class movement since the war—this is actually the first indication we have observed so far that there may exist cumulative elements in explosions of consciousness. It has not disappeared from view subsequently— Durand (in Dubois *et al.* 1971, p. 11) notes that in a not-untypical day in November 1969 *Le Monde* reported that no less than seven French factories were occupied by their workers, while in March 1972 around 100,000 French workers, mostly young, took part in the funeral procession of the 'gauchist' shot at Renault, in defiance of the C.G.T. The occupations, and democratic worker committees, have also been an increasing feature of Italian industrial relations since Italy's 'long hot summer' of 1968.

Why these signs of increasing consciousness at such a late stage in the development of capitalism? Will it increase further? These are the questions we must now consider. Some Marxists answer with very general economic theories of neo-capitalist society. In their view, the proletariat revolution will occur when capitalism has reached its limit of world-wide expansion. Only then will the contradiction between production and consumption and the falling rate of profit produce the kind of economic crisis predicted by Marx. Yet it is difficult to link this to the relative instability of France and Italy, societies characterised by uneven economic development and a relatively weak capitalist sector. Furthermore, this theory neglects two apparently salient features of the May events, the part played in them by technical and scientific workers and that played by students. To analyse these factors we must turn to theories of 'the new working class'.

7. THE NEW WORKING CLASS AND THE PRODUCTION OF KNOWLEDGE

The main theorists considered in this section are the French sociologists Alain Touraine and Serge Mallet. Though their arguments overlap, they are not identical. Their writings are ambiguous in several ways, and Touraine seems also to have shifted his ground in recent years.[1] Hence, though I will present the theory of the new working class as a simple, coherent entity, this is very much a composite and manufactured theory (comparable to that of Posner 1970).

In its boldest form the theory of the new working class asserts that Western society is about to move into a new 'post-industrial' or 'post-capitalist' era (Touraine 1971). This era will be dominated by a new force of production—*knowledge*. The key factor for social development is no longer capital, but the production and application of scientific and technical knowledge. Hence, the key, problematic social relations are no longer those contained within the manufacturing process itself (between capitalist and worker), but those arising from the production of knowledge. This involves two major institutional areas of society—universities, and science-based industries and government departments. We are therefore immediately offered an explanation of why both students and technical and scientific workers contributed to the May movement: they form a new, progressive working class concerned to contest the power of the archaic capitalist state.

I have not the space here to consider the theory in its most general implication for society.[2] Instead, I will merely note some

[1] Mallet has himself observed this shift: 'L'itinéraire d'Alain Touraine' in *L'Homme et la Société* (1970).
[2] To date, Daniel Bell (1971) has been the most thorough investigator of the theory of 'post-industrial society'. As he notes, it

55

of the difficulties confronting it in its specific applications to the student movement and to the technical–scientific worker. Applied to the student movement, it involves a very materialist theory of unrest, emphasising the increase in student numbers, bureaucratisation, government intervention and links with the military–industrial complex and with the occupational needs of the economy. Yet most of these features are least pronounced in the academic subjects from which the radicals are disproportionately drawn, the liberal arts and the social sciences. Furthermore, this leaves unexplained some very salient features of the student movement—the over-representation of the children of liberal professionals, its cultural and artistic elements and its overt concern with the liberal, humane values of the West. This is a movement located largely in the realm of ideas, disproportionately composed of those with access to the cultural 'superstructure' of society. The social contradiction seems here to be less between the technology of knowledge and private property than between the technocratic and cultural functions of education. Certainly, this contradiction is most directly felt in sociology itself, continually torn between its tradition of practical service to existing society and its mission to pursue basic humanitarian values. And it is sociology students who are the most radical.[1]

The students did, of course, spark off the May 1968 events, but was their movement really connected to the workers' movement by anything more than a common experience, heightened

---

must clarify four issues: (1) the scope and limits of technical expertise in solving social problems; (2) an assessment of the new knowledge-based industries; (3) the basis of class solidarity among highly-skilled workers; (4) the likelihood of technicians and technocrats becoming the dominant class. I confine myself here to certain aspects of (3) and (4).

[1] The literature on the student movement is voluminous. Good analyses, though from very different viewpoints, together with extensive bibliographies, can be found in S. M. Lipset, *Rebellion in the University* (Boston: Little, Brown & Co., 1972), and M. W. Miles, *The Radical Probe: The Logic of Student Rebellion* (New York: Atheneum, 1971). Touraine (1968) does not ignore these points, but their place in his largely 'materialist' theory is somewhat unclear.

in France, of police repression? Studies show that the connection between students and workers was minimal—for example, in the Dubois *et al.* sample (1971, p. 370), only 6·5 per cent of striking factories entered into any discussion with the students. As one of the authors, Vidal, concludes (p. 547), the students' and workers' movements were analogous but not identical. They were based on different social contradictions, and no dialectic was set up between them. Links between the students and some of the technical–scientific workers were slightly stronger, and I will return to this later. For the most part, however, the student movement was separate in origins, personnel and aims, a characteristic even more pronounced in other Western countries.

A more interesting and plausible application of the theory of the new working class is to the workers of the technologically advanced and highly automated industries. The 'new working class' is composed of technically-trained manual workers, technicians and certain of the *cadres* of managers and engineers. Hence it transcends the traditional manual–non-manual dividing line, and also that within the working class between skilled and unskilled workers—for 'technically-trained manual workers' covers skilled and semi-skilled alike. It is located in the most advanced and automated sector of the economy, in the chemical processing industries (chemicals, gas, oil, some foodstuffs), advanced engineering (machine tools and electrical engineering), electronics, atomic energy and sundry other innovating areas of industry. In varying degrees, these workers have polyvalent technical and scientific skills usually denied to the general managers and capitalists who control them in industry.

To the British or American reader it might seem rather startling that automated production should be thought to generate increased class consciousness, for almost all English-speaking authors have stressed its 'harmonising' effects. They stress four such effects: the re-introduction of the cohesive work-group into industry, the increase in job satisfaction, better fringe benefits and conditions of employment (often including the granting of staff status to manual workers) and more amicable industrial relations. In another study (1973) I have reviewed their findings and presented evidence of my own to suggest that the most significant improvement conferred by automated production is an increased level of financial security. This might seem a formidable list of causes of a *decline* in class conflict in industry; however, by rejecting only the fourth effect (more amicable industrial relations), contemporary French writers have claimed that automation will increase working-class consciousness by stimulating what has been termed *conflictual participation*.

Mallet, for example, accepts that automated production increases both the job satisfaction and the material prosperity of the worker. Outside of the plant he is now a full member of the high-consumption society of advanced capitalism. But, he argues, workers are still distinguishable from other classes by the fundamental criterion, 'that of exercising a productive role but being excluded from ownership or control of the instruments of production which they serve' (1963, p. 19). This is alienation not *in* work but *from* work, a deprivation which becomes clearer than ever to the workers by virtue of their changed production role. Here Touraine develops the argument more fully. In the automated plant, the real centre of power in the organisation is no longer hidden from the worker by many levels of superior authority, each with its own discretionary rights. Now, all decision-making processes are integrated into a central system of communication and control, of which the parts (and therefore the employees) are highly interdependent. The analogy is with cybernetics: the plant may be viewed as an information system, centrally programmed. But the factory is not technically 'neutral': it is a system of class power, and the worker's subordination to the 'programmer', the capitalist, is clearly revealed to him. Issues of control and alienation become more salient, the workers possess more control, and working-class action is less likely to be fobbed off with economism. The high interdependence makes him more than ever a participant of the organisation, but his subordination renders this 'conflictual participation'. Furthermore, different companies are also more interdependent within the economy of advanced capitalism, and conflict within the company must be more closely linked to global conflict than hitherto.

Implicit in Mallet's view and explicit in Touraine's is the notion that a class which seeks to transform society must be deeply implicated in that society. Touraine links this to his three-stage model of the development of technology and class consciousness. In stage A, craft production, the workers attain a high consciousness of their own group identity. In stage B, mass production, they add to this a recognition of their opponent, the employer, and his system of management control. In stage C, automated production, their sense of conflict is widened and transferred to the total, societal, level. In the first and second stages working-class consciousness, however militant, views the developing industrial society *from outside*. It is supported by the values of the pre-existing craft and/or working-class community, and resists the encroachments of large-scale industrialisation. This is a conventional view of craft unions, but Touraine applies it equally to the most militant working-class movements of the mass production era. They are doomed to failure in their revolutionary aims because they really reject not just the relations of production, but also the emerging forces of production. They are truly reactionary, and have no viable alternative society to offer the worker. By contrast, the identity of the worker in the advanced technologies is conferred from within both the new system of production and the new 'industrial civilisation' of mass consumption. He is reacting not against these modern features of society, but against the antiquated system of industrial control based on private property. He thus represents the emergent forces of production against the traditional, capitalist relations of production (Touraine 1966, pp. 322–3; 1968, Ch. 1 and pp. 157–63; Mallet 1963, pp. 12–13, 62, 171).

This is a remarkable twist of the Marxist tail. It restores the materialist dialectic to Marxist theory by focusing once more on what Marx saw as the central contradiction of capitalism: the emergence of the collective forces amidst the individual relations of production. It re-establishes the working class as the standard-bearers of the new society. It purges class conflicts of their 'sentimental' aspects (Mallet's phrase) and makes them a simple issue of control over the means of production. This in itself weakens the traditional hostility between manual and non-manual workers, and reveals to workers, technicians, and engineers alike their collective interests against the wielders of industrial power, private capital. Finally, by stressing the new organisational power of the worker, it may reduce the dependence of contemporary Marxism on the somewhat dubious 'explosion of consciousness': the collective experience of the worker occurs not only during strike situations but in the very process of production. All these apparent advantages make this a very attractive theory for the more alert Marxists, and they have appropriated various elements of it, especially in analysing the events of May 1968 (Garaudy 1970; Gorz 1969; Posner 1970).

One of the most surprising characteristics of May 1968 was the participation in the factory strikes and occupations of hitherto quiescent workers, technicians and even managers in the electronics industry, in Electricité de France, in chemicals, in petrochemicals and even in the atomic energy establishments of the French government. Their factory occupations were not among the most frequent or violent—for the traditional engineering sectors were dominant overall (Adam 1970)—but in many instances they were more innovative than the 'traditional' workers. Durand has shown that they were more likely to set up General Assemblies and Worker Commissions to discuss self management. He concludes that the technicians and engineers:

> . . . rely on their occupational standing to denounce and break the constraints of the system. This recalls the role which craftsmen played in the working-class movement at the birth of the technical rationalisation of production. Before the new constraints of the system of intellectual production, the central groups in the production process defend their professional autonomy and their rights to responsibility and collective control—self-management by the producers. (in Dubois *et al.* 1971, p. 158)

What seems especially interesting about these groups is their concern with an *alternative* system of industrial control, the very element which was usually lacking among traditional workers. Does this mean, therefore, that the 'new working class' is more likely than the old to attain full class consciousness? I will consider the other elements of consciousness.

A sense of class *identity* is usually well developed among 'traditional' workers, as we have seen. Yet this element is com-

60

paratively weak among the new working class. Even without the students this is a very heterogeneous group, and traditional occupational and status groups within it remain distinctive. On close investigation, the participation of the *cadres* in May was negligible, apart from some young engineers. Lower production managers generally changed sides after the initial surge of conflict, finding they had more in common with the employer than with the workers. Among the *cadres*, the movement has apparently died away (Dulong, in Dubois *et al.* 1971).

Technical and scientific workers were more heavily involved, but were nevertheless aware of the contrary pressures upon them. Some of the more radical ones formed close links with the students. The atomic energy workers, for example, were the group most affected by student propaganda stressing the need for the abolition of bureaucracy in society (Tripier 1970). Yet the organisation that acted as spokesman for most of these groups, the C.F.D.T., became aware of the gap between their slogans of 'self-management' and the traditional workers' cries for 'workers' power' (Durand, in Dubois *et al.* 1971). The language and demands of traditional and new workers differed. The latter had either a distinctive sense of their own identity, but as a *middle* class (i.e. between workers and management), or a fuzzier notion of unity with the working class. The ambiguity hampered the emergence of a sense of working-class *identity*, and presumably will do so at least as long as 'traditional' workers remain a sizeable part of the population of Western countries.

The next element to consider is that of *totality*. (I wish to leave the question of conflict or opposition until later.) To what extent do 'new' workers consider themselves and their social situation to be defined by their productive situation? Touraine has shown in his inter-industry study that workers in advanced industries are much less likely to be embedded in exclusively working-class residential communities. He links this to his theory that they are now participating in society in its post-industrial phase rather than protecting themselves against it (1966, pp. 199–205). Yet if workers' interests are focused on the control of their own firm, and are not reinforced by experiences in working-class communities, why should they concern themselves with the interests of workers in other firms? Mallet (1963) admits (pp. 60–6) that automated technologies contain pressures toward a narrow plant unionism, but argues that such 'fractionalisation' of the working class may be counteracted by the high interdependence of firms in the advanced sector of the economy. Yet one group of writers has observed that the most novel aspect of the May 1968 events was the crisis within the industrial enterprise, and that only the traditional global interests of French unions prevented this from causing a decline in national grievances (Reynaud *et al.* 1971). In this they are supported by the insistence of contemporary radical economists that the modern corporation has increasing independence from the market. Furthermore, and this is a possibility that no writer has mentioned, it may be that the *employer's* class solidarity is also weakened in advanced technologies. I have elsewhere noted (1973, Ch. 10) the high interdependence between employer and worker in automated production. The worker's co-operation is more necessary than ever before, for the plant is too costly to be left idle or to be sabotaged. Training replacements is also costly. In such circumstances, employers are more willing to buy off discontent and to treat separately with their work-force. If French employers began plant bargaining, much of the heat of French industrial relations would be removed. *Plant unionism* would thus weaken class conflict on both sides.

However, a French study of militants provides some supporting evidence for the Mallet–Touraine position on this issue. The authors classify six types of trade union action on the basis of their respondents' answers to a large number of questions. I will mention only three of these here: B_2, class unionism (the most militant of the traditional forms of trade unionism); C_2, plant bargaining; and C_3, which I shall term 'macro control' (the French term is *syndicalisme gestionnaire*, but it covers wider issues than mere workplace control). C_2 and C_3 represent the two main forms of union described by Mallet and Touraine in automated industries. The former may weaken class solidarity, the latter would not. According to their theory, both C_2 and C_3 should increase with automation, but the latter much more so. This is precisely what does happen, as we can see opposite.

Stage of production	Class unionism (B₂)	Plant bargaining (C₂)	Macro control (C₃)	
Craft	38%	10%	20%	(=100%)
Mass	31%	12%	19%	(=100%)
Automated	30%	19%	35%	(=100%)

Source: C. Durand (1968), table 1, p. 130.

C_3 is in fact the most popular of the six types among the militants in automated production. It appears, then, that the new working class is not as yet fractionalised by plant bargaining. This may indicate a conflict between the new industrial exigencies of employers and workers and their traditional class-conscious habits. From past French experience, which I described earlier, there is no necessary reason why the former should triumph. The sense of totality remains surprisingly acute.

The sense of opposition is more problematic, however. Ambiguities are apparent in the writings of both Mallet and Touraine. While asserting that conflict will increase in scope and intensity, they also note that automation speeds the 'integration' of the working class into advanced industrial society. Mallet (1963), for example, suggests that the automated plant becomes '. . . the privileged place in which the worker can integrate himself into an economic society from which he has been hitherto excluded' (p. 261). Of course, it may be over-concern with traditional Marxism which leads us to expect a proletarian revolution, if it comes at all, to come from an excluded class overturning the system, rather than from integrative processes. I have already noted Touraine's argument against this. But there is evidence from the Durand study to suggest that the integrative processes may actually cause a decline in conflict intensity. The questions put to the workers in this study were in the form of sets of six alternative statements (corresponding to the union types), from which they had to choose one or two from each set. If we compare the B_2 statements (traditional class unionism) with the C_3 ones (the more conflictual of the two automation types) we find that they differ on two main criteria. The first is the Tourainian one of modernity: B_2 rejects company mergers while C_3 welcomes them, for example. But the second is the relative importance given to conflict. On wages policy, whereas B_2 views differentials as a way of dividing the working class and thus emphasises redistribution, C_3 emphasises the need to stimulate the economy as a whole, and thus to increase the total cake available for distribution. Whereas B_2 rejects participation in national commissions as class collaboration, C_3 accepts the need to participate and influence. Whereas B_2 rejects any incomes policy in a society based on profit, C_3 merely considers that incomes policy cannot be separated from general economic planning. In short, C_3 endorses *bargaining*, but at a national level. If the worker in the automated sector is to inaugurate a collective era of production, it seems more likely to be what Banks (1970) has termed 'voluntary collectivism' rather than the dictatorship of the proletariat.

In May 1968 this ambiguity emerged in the 'new working class' movement. The consciousness which emerged during the May events is not readily reducible to traditional modes of class conflict. We look in vain among the technicians and *cadres* for traditional anti-capitalist and solidaristic working-class sentiments. 'Surplus value', 'class exploitation' and even the word 'revolution' itself are notably absent from their propaganda. Instead we find the key term, *auto-gestion*, self-management and a concern to work out procedures to ensure democratic control of decision-making processes. The novel nature of their concerns, and the lack of guidance they obtained from existing political and industrial organisations, gives them a confused non-ideological tone. In one electronics firm the workers, technicians and engineers voiced a general demand '*Vouloir et construire une société plus juste*', expressed in the strongest of terms, but they worked out a detailed programme by which employees would be consulted only on issues directly concerning their own narrow field of competence.[1] The writings of some of the *cadres'* Work

[1] J. Leenhardt, 'La nouvelle classe ouvrière en grève', *Sociologie du Travail*, x (1968). It is worth noting that Goldthorpe *et al.* (1969, p. 187) give a very misleading account of this study, which they claim '. . . shows that the aims of demands for *cogestion* was essentially to increase operating efficiency and profitability so as to

64

Commissions quoted Trotsky alongside management consultants (Reynaud *et al.* 1971). The atomic energy workers aimed at control, not only of their own work, but of the application of their knowledge in the wider society—yet they were aware of their inability to work out practicable schemes to effect this (Tripier 1970). 'Conflictual participation' contains its own contradictions, and the new working class can be revolutionary only by jettisoning the participation.

The weakness of the sense of opposition can now be linked to a problem that should have already occurred to most readers: why is this new working class confined to France? For it appears to produce little echo elsewhere. In Britain Clive Jenkins's union appears to be the only novel element of militancy among scientific and technical workers. In the United States *one* strike among research workers at M.I.T. is produced as evidence for the new movement there (Garaudy 1970, p. 65). How can this be a movement characteristic of advanced capitalism in general? Touraine is aware of this problem and answers it by pointing to France's 'archaism', which paradoxically puts her in the vanguard of progress. The emerging social group is thrust into conflict relations with the capitalist state earlier than will happen in other countries. Almost alone of the Western countries, France (like Italy) has still not solved the problem of the traditional working class. New demands generated by technological change are channelled into the old class-warfare institutions—only in this way could the students, the traditional workers and the technical–scientific workers be linked through vaguely socialist ideals and tactics. The link has not occurred elsewhere. But is the link in France coincidental, or is it a pointer to the future?

One factor to be considered is social mobility. The French equivalent of lower and middle management, the *cadres*, have been generally denied access to positions of high authority in industry (and in society at large) by the close-knit nature of the French ruling class dominated by inherited wealth and *les*

---

make possible higher wage and salary levels for all employees'. Leenhardt, in fact, stresses the non-economic nature of the demands. Nor does the other study (Barrier 1968) referred to by *The Affluent Worker* authors, go as directly anti-Mallet as they claim.

Grandes Écoles. We can assume that blocked mobility and grievances concerning class barriers among the 'new working class' are more frequent in France than elsewhere (Reynaud *et al.* 1971). A study of technicians and engineers in the French electricity industry has shown that union militancy is positively related to experience of blocked mobility, whereas the opposite is the case with manual workers (Barrier 1968). It is possible that such blockages will be more frequent in 'post-industrial society' than hitherto, with a growing barrier between those with generalist, university education and those with specialised technical qualifications, and this might increase the sense of class identity and opposition of the latter. But in so far as it does, it will divide them from the graduates and split Touraine's new class into two. The stratification system may thus retain its complexity and hinder the simple polarisation of society. If blocked mobility is not more frequent, then the initial conflict between worker and employer will be weaker. Either way, we reach a less dramatic conclusion than Touraine or Mallet.

Another indication that the sense of class opposition may be weaker than suggested among the 'new working class' is provided by trends in trade-union membership. In most Western countries, the proportion of union members among white-collar and white-coat workers is static or rising only very slowly. The main growth area is in public employment, where employers are less hostile to unionism. Such employer encouragement diminishes the usefulness of white-collar unionisation rates as an index of class conflict.[1] This is supported by current research which shows that in England staff and professional associations are increasing their membership at a far higher rate than are non-manual trade unions. The activities of these associations vary from full-scale negotiations about wages and job control with employers, through attempts to control qualifications (and so to restrict entry to the occupation) to very mild forms of action such as giving advice on contracts and publishing salary surveys. It is the

[1] G. S. Bain, *The Growth of White Collar Unionism* (Oxford University Press, 1970); W. Ginsburg, 'Review of literature on union growth, government and structure—1955–1969', *Review of Industrial Relations Research*, I (1970). The level of white-collar unionism is disproportionately high in France, however.

mildest type which is growing fastest.[1] This growth may be parallel to the more dramatic French developments, indicating the emergence of intermediate occupational groups with distinctive work situations and interests. But it is a far cry from the new working class. Participation rather than conflict seems the dominating issue, and where conflict does arise it is sectional rather than class conflict. The British Medical Association might be just as appropriate a model as the C.F.D.T. for the new working class outside France.

I have cast a fairly sceptical eye over the theory of the new working class. Despite its attractions, two main reservations must be made. Firstly, all four elements of class consciousness seem to depend critically on factors not incorporated in the theory and, indeed, external to the necessary employment relationship of the new working class. If the French new workers are relatively class-conscious, this is largely due to the 'archaism' of France, to the reinforcing effects of traditional and idiosyncratic contradictions. Without this reinforcement it is doubtful whether the conflict between 'new workers' and their employers can be elevated to the status of a major 'contradiction'. Why should it be a more important source of instability than differences of age, sex, religion or other sources of tension in modern society? Here we surely move to a multi-factor explanation of social conflict—and not to an expectation of revolution. Secondly, even in France, the new workers' sense of *opposition* and *identity* is relatively weak despite apparent concern with a restructuring of the total society. This is precisely the opposite revolutionary failing of the traditional working class, strong on identity and opposition, weak on totality and alternatives. Yet it gives the new working class the same quality of utopianism, the same failure to translate a mixed consciousness into a consistent series of radical actions.

[1] Research conducted in the Cambridge University Department of Applied Economics by R. M. Blackburn, K. Prandy and A. Stewart: an unpublished paper by Blackburn, 'Developments in Staff Associations' (1969).

8. CONCLUSION

Before turning to more complex questions of theory we can quickly dismiss the harmonistic tinge of the more extreme versions of 'the end of ideology' thesis. Even relatively successful bargaining between employer and worker does not answer all the important needs of workers. Whatever other industrial attitudes they may hold, workers show unmistakable signs of conscious deprivation which we might well wish to term *alienation*. This holds for all the countries we have examined.

Yet alienation does not express the worker's total consciousness or explain his behaviour fully. Indeed, at every turn we have been confronted by a profound *dualism* in the worker's situation and his consciousness. Co-existing with a normally passive sense of alienation is an experience of (largely economic) interdependence with the employer at a factual, if not a normative, level. Surges of class consciousness are continually undercut by economism, and capitalism survives. Yet this is a much less even and harmonistic process than 'the end of ideology' implies. There is a distinct lack of fit between the two halves of consciousness, producing erratic and often chaotic industrial relations punctuated by genuine 'explosions' of consciousness. Action cannot be consistent when consciousness is contradictory, and this is the obstacle to revolution as well as to harmony.

In short, we must reject both rival claims that the Capital–Labour relationship contains an inherent tendency toward either revolution or harmonistic stability. Once we do this, we can see that the 'end of ideology' theorists have practised a sleight-of-hand (I hope an unconscious one) upon us. While correctly pointing out the way in which extra-industrial factors have heightened class conflict in countries like France or Italy, they have drawn attention away from the fact that the relative industrial peace of countries such as the United States may be equally

68

produced by extra-industrial causes (such as, for example, racial divisions in the American working class). A genuine multi-factor explanation is needed on this side, too. The damage done to Marxism is even more evident, for we have seen that the Marxist theory of the dialectical progression of class consciousness does not work. The four elements I isolated—identity, opposition, totality and alternative—are indeed separable in reality and can occur, in varying degrees, without the others. In all the situations I have described, at least one of the elements has been relatively lacking.

Among manual workers in traditional industries a realistic appraisal of alternative structures is lacking even among the most class-conscious workers in the most explosive situations. Whatever the *objective* possibility that they might be the bearers of a new principle of social structure—collectivism—they themselves either do not perceive this or do not know how to translate it into action. Collectivism more often means for them collective *identity*. The explosion of consciousness is trapped in a vicious circle (from identity to opponent to totality, and then back to identity), and so does not make a revolution.

Among the new working class in advanced sectors of production the possibilities for action are still more open, and conclusions are more susceptible to the hazards of crystal-gazing. At its most class-conscious peak hitherto in France, appraisal of alternative structures is now developing further than among the traditional working class. Yet this is accompanied by a less developed sense of class identity and opposition, and bears upon the essential ambiguity of the desire for 'conflictual participation'. Outside France this has implied far more participation than conflict. The evidence appears to bear out the Mallet–Touraine thesis that control issues will replace quantitative economic issues as the dominating element in industrial relations. This would bring distributive rather than collective aspects of power to the fore, making it more difficult to solve conflict by compromise. Yet even such 'zero-sum' aspects of power *can* be compromised, and if both employer and new working class start off with a predisposition toward joint participation rather than class conflict, then we might expect compromise to be the result. Overall, it seems safer to expect intermediate forms of class relations rather than either revolution or near-harmony.

Analysis of both the new and the traditional working class has revealed a fatal contradiction within the working-class movement. Those who are most alienated and most desperate are those who are least confident of their ability to change their situation. Those who are most confident in their own power and clearest in their intentions feel least embattled and disposed towards desperate remedies. We might also add that the most alienated have, objectively, the least to offer society as a whole: in Marx's sense, they are least progressive. Are we to view a revolutionary class as alienated or self-confident? The ambiguity has remained not just in the realm of ideas, but in the material world too.

It is, of course, a possibility that capitalism will be unable to supply the mass of the population with the material prosperity that supports economism. At the time of writing both increasing structural unemployment and the Western nations' difficulties in reaching a joint monetary policy make this a distinct possibility. In that case we should expect a genuine explosion of industrially-based social conflict (in which demand for some form of social control over the economy would doubtless be heard).[1] Yet there are two great obstacles against this being a cumulative process of class consciousness toward *socialism*. Firstly, the same economic trends threaten to divide the working class both nationally and internationally. In almost all Western countries now, those who would be worst hit by recession are disproportionately drawn from distinct ethnic, religious or cultural sub-groups within the working class. Blacks in the United States, coloured immigrants, Celts and Catholics in the United Kingdom, southern Europeans in Northern Europe, southerners in Italy—hardship among all these groups would not necessarily stir the working class as a whole into action.[2] Furthermore, the response to an interna-

---

[1] A study of 114 nations in the 1960s found a remarkably high correlation of 0·44 between measures of short-term economic deprivation and the degree of civil strife: T. Gurr, 'A Causal Model of Civil Strife: A Comparative Analysis Using New Indices', *American Political Science Review*, LXII (1968).

[2] Marx himself stressed the ethnic antagonism between Irish and English workers in nineteenth-century Britain. He wrote: 'This antagonism is the *secret of the impotence of the English working class*'

tional crisis might be further economic nationalism, in which some countries would eventually go to the wall. We can already see that nationalism and racialism have driven the U.S. labour movement to the right rather than the left.

This raises the second obstacle. Socialism is a philosophy which is *learned*. It does not suddenly and spontaneously explode within the working class; rather, it is the product of two factors, the continuous experience of the worker in his productive life and the interpretation of this experience by organised groups over a considerable period of time. Where the experience and the actions of organisations directly transmitting this experience are dualistic, no consistent dialectical process can emerge. The importance of revolutionary traditions in France and Italy has been demonstrated in this book: without them it is improbable that working-class protest can be directed toward the creation of a new society. And even with them that protest has actually to *counteract* the pressure toward compromise generated by existing collective organisations.

At various points in this book I have noted the importance of national differences within capitalism. If I am now concluding that working-class revolutionary consciousness is unlikely to develop in most capitalist countries, this carries with it the implication that the working class does not carry within itself a new form of social order. Marx was surely right in observing that the major contradiction of capitalist society was between the individual interests of capitalists and the collective interest of the working and consuming population. He was also correct in pointing out the working class's inherent drive toward collective identity and organisation. Yet these two trends need not converge in a proletarian revolution. If the working class and its organisations accept as the framework for part of their activities an economism that does not challenge the structure of capitalism, then their collectivism does not escalate into an aggressive socie-

---

(his emphasis) in a letter to A. Meyer and A. Vogt in 1870: *Selected Correspondence* edn (Moscow: Progress Publishers, 1955) 237. These divisions parallel those I mentioned above—those most desperately affected by the economic system (in this case, the minorities) are least able to offer a progressive solution to it.

71

tal force but turns in upon itself. The 'dialectic' of class consciousness is circular, not progressive.[1] In this situation the task of imposing some degree of collectivism over the society as a whole is left to the capitalist class through the emergence of the corporation, the institutionalised money market and Keynesian state economics. The collectivist 'revolution' may be upon us already, but without the working class (cf. Banks 1970).

This brings us, finally, to the problem of the Marxist theory of revolution as a whole. The most revolutionary situations seem to be those in which *several* contradictions rend society at once. In the contemporary West I have examined three types of contradiction: that between employer and worker; that contained within the economic sector between advanced and 'archaic' social managements; and that between different sectors of society (in this case, between the economic and the cultural spheres as they affect education). It is where these contradictions reinforce each other, as in contemporary France, that we come closest to a revolutionary situation. Revolution might thus be a product of uneven development in both the economic and the non-economic sectors, of multiple contradictions and social chaos, rather than of the stark societal class confrontation envisaged by Marx.

We would do well to consider the *consequences* of such revolutionary situations. Marxism is a fundamentally optimistic social theory because it portrays the revolutionary class armed with a new progressive principle of social development—capital and individual enterprise in the case of the bourgeoisie, collectivism and planning in the case of the proletariat. But if the class that leads a revolution is smaller, less confident and endowed with strange but necessary allies by the forces of uneven development, then a rather less optimistic vista opens up before the revolutionaries. Either they might be defeated because of an inability to comprehend the complexities of such a situation—as happened

[1] Sometimes a change in *tactics* gives the impression of progression. Such is the illusion created in France and Italy whenever there is an outbreak of political strikes. The contemporary wave of factory occupations in Britain is extending the range of reformist demands to 'the right to work', but this is no more revolutionary than traditional union attemps to restrict the free market for labour in other ways.

in France in the 1790s when the rising bourgeoisie, the radical *sans-culottes* and the poor peasants failed to find a policy that might unite their interests (Moore 1969, Ch. 2). Or they might be victorious, but only at the cost of imposing a dictatorship over allies and enemies alike—as the Bolsheviks succeeded in doing. Though contemporary France and Italy may in some senses provide a revolutionary situation, it is a long way from there to a successful revolution. The events of May 1968 turned into the débâcle of June and July because the opponents of revolution were very much more united than the various groups who found themselves labelled as revolutionaries. It is sometimes argued that European Communist parties are so unresponsive to popular and radical discontent precisely because they perceive the nature of the contradictions produced by uneven development within their supporters and potential supporters.[1] Perhaps a genuine Leninist dictatorship of the proletariat *is* the only revolutionary way out of the impasse. Yet this is a far cry from classical Marxism and from the optimism of most radical views of revolution. Perhaps revolutions in the Marxist sense *never* occur. Those situations in which the social structure has been transformed from top to bottom by the replacement of one hegemonic class by another may only look 'revolutionary' with hindsight. To contemporaries, the replacement of landowners by capitalists in countries like Britain or Japan seemed a relatively peaceful process of class assimilation. In the modern West the major possibilities seem to be either a comparable process of assimilation between 'capitalists', 'managers' and 'technocrats', or a *coup d'état* carried out during a period of social confusion in the name of the proletariat (or—and this may be more likely—a Fascist *coup* to forestall the latter eventuality). It seems rather unlikely that the proletariat carries *in itself* the power to be a class *for itself*.

[1] C. Macridis, 'The immobility of the French Communist Party', *Journal of Politics*, xx (1958).

BIBLIOGRAPHY

G. Adam, 'Etude statistique des grèves de mai-juin 1968', *Revue française de science politique*, xx (1970). Contains the most accurate French data available on the distribution of strikes by industry.

L. Althusser, *For Marx* (London: Allen Lane The Penguin Press, 1969). Chapters 3 and 6 contain an interesting, though unnecessarily obscure, attempt to steer Marxism toward multi-causality.

C. Argyris, *Personality and Organization* (New York: Harper & Row, 1964). A human relations approach to the discrepancy between the needs of the 'mature, healthy personality' and the nature of lower-class employment.

J. A. Banks, *Marxist Sociology in Action* (London: Faber & Faber, 1970). A test of Marxist theories of industrial relations (of a rather old-fashioned kind) with data from the British mining and iron and steel industries.

C. Barrier, 'Techniciens et grèves à l'Electricité de France', *Sociologie du Travail*, x (1968). Sample of workers, technicians and engineers, and their level of militancy related to indices of social mobility.

D. Bell, *The End of Ideology* (New York: Collier Books paperback edition, 1961). A classic, containing much of interest on U.S. labour history, even if we reject the 'end of ideology' thesis.

——, 'The post-industrial society: the evolution of an idea', *Survey*, xvii (1971). Review of theories of post-industrial society from Marx onward. A general schema of Bell's own views is outlined at the end, and we are promised a full-scale work later.

Robin Blackburn, 'The Unequal Society' in Blackburn and A. Cockburn, *The Incompatibles: Trade Union Militancy and the Consensus* (Harmondsworth, Middlesex: Penguin Books, 1967). Interesting data on inequality in employment combined with an unconvincing polemic against *The Affluent Worker* study.

R. Blauner, *Alienation and freedom: the factory worker and his industry* (Chicago: University of Chicago Press, 1964). Bold attempt to operationalise 'alienation' and relate it to technological change in industry.

P. Blumberg, *Industrial Democracy: the Sociology of Participation* (London: Constable, 1968). A somewhat optimistic view of industrial democracy from the Hawthorne studies to the Yugoslav experiments.

T. Cliff and C. Barker, *Incomes Policy legislation and Shop Stewards* (Harrow, Middlesex: London Industrial Shop Stewards Defence Committee, 1966). Effective socialist polemic against incomes policy, productivity deals and other seducers of the working class.

R. Dubin, 'Industrial workers' worlds: a study of the central life interests of industrial workers', *Social Problems*, III (1956). Study of American workers, claiming that their central life interests lie outside of work. But see my discussion above.

P. Dubois, R. Dulong, C. Durand, S. Erbès-Seguin and D. Vidal, *Grèves Revendicatives ou Grèves Politiques?* (Paris: Éditions Anthropos, 1971). The most detailed account yet of the factory occupations of May–June 1968, relying on several samples of activists and factories. Durand provides a comparison of 'traditional' and 'new' workers. Dulong looks sceptically at the *cadres* movement. Erbès-Seguin looks at the relations between unions and workers. Dubois analyses the organisational forms of the occupation in a large sample of 182 factories. Vidal gives an Althusserian view of French social contradictions.

C. Durand, 'La signification professionnelle et économique de l'action syndicale', *Sociologie du Travail*, x (1968). A special issue of the journal reports on the C.N.R.S. study of French union activists. Durand presents interesting data relating attitudes to technology, type of ownership, etc.

R. Garaudy, *The Turning Point of Socialism* (London: Fontana Books, 1970). A Marxist view of the 'post-industrial society', sufficiently original to lead to Garaudy's expulsion from the French Communist Party.

J. H. Goldthorpe, D. Lockwood, F. Bechhofer and J. Platt, *The Affluent Worker: Industrial Attitudes and Behaviour* (1968); *The Affluent Worker in the Class Structure* (Cambridge University Press, 1969). Vols. 1 and 3 of the most important study yet conducted by British industrial sociologists. Note, however, that the data presented in vol. 1 do not unequivocally support the authors' theory of 'orientations to work'.

A. Gorz, *Réforme et Révolution* (Paris: Éditions du Seuil, 1969). What tactics should French socialists adopt after May 1968? A revised and extended edition of *Stratégie ouvrière et néocapitalisme* (Paris: Éditions du Seuil, 1963), of which a section was translated as 'Work and Consumption' in P. Anderson *et al.*, *Towards Socialism* (London: Fontana Books, 1965).

R. F. Hamilton, *Affluence and the French Worker in the Fourth Republic* (Princeton, New Jersey: Princeton University Press, 1967). Good secondary analysis of French data relevant to the *embourgeoisement* thesis. Especially valuable for the reader confined to studies in English.

E. J. Hiller, *The Strike* (Chicago University Press, 1928). A classic and neglected study of strikes in Britain and the U.S., concentrating on the worker's view of the strike.

D. L. Horowitz, *The Italian Labor Movement* (Cambridge, Massachusetts: Harvard University Press, 1963). Standard historical account.

R. Hyman, *Marxism and the Sociology of Trade Unionism* (London: Pluto Press, 1971). Review of Marxist theory. Especially useful for setting Lenin's remarks on 'trade union consciousness' in context, and for an understanding of 'dual power'.

C. Kerr, J. T. Dunlop, F. H. Harbison, and C. A. Myers, *Industrialism and Industrial Man*, 2nd edn (London: Heinemann, 1962). Bold generalisations about the past and future course of industrialisation in the world. In the 'end of ideology' tradition, and easily open to attack. The so-called 'logic of industrialism' is somewhat elusive.

A. Kornhauser, *The Mental Health of the Industrial Worker*

(New York: John Wiley, 1965). The richest data published on the American worker. The author's composite indices of satisfaction, mental health, etc., are sometimes of dubious validity, but can be decomposed again by the reader.

Tony Lane and Ken Roberts, *Strike at Pilkingtons* (London: Fontana Books, 1971). A vivid yet sensible account of an explosive, unofficial strike.

J. C. Leggett, *Class, Race and Labor* (New York: Oxford University Press, 1968). Study of class consciousness among Detroit workers. Good data, though not always supporting the author's quasi-Marxist interpretation.

S. M. Lipset, 'The changing class structure and contemporary European politics', *Daedelus*, XCIII (1964). An 'end of ideology' viewpoint, useful but over-argued.

S. Mallet, *La nouvelle classe ouvrière* (Paris: Éditions du Seuil, 1963). The source of the 'new working class' debate. Impressionistic account of a few technologically advanced French firms.

M. Mann, 'The social cohesion of liberal democracy', *American Sociological Review*, XXXV (1970). Secondary analysis of attitudes in Britain and the United States. Social cohesion depends on the lack of consistent commitment to general values of any sort and on 'pragmatic acceptance' on the part of the working class.

——, *Workers on the Move: the Sociology of Relocation* (Cambridge University Press, 1973). A factory relocation is used as a critical test of commitment to work and non-work areas of life at different levels of technology.

B. Moore, *Social Origins of Dictatorship and Democracy* (Harmondsworth, Middlesex: Penguin Books, 1969). A historical materialist explanation of modern social and political systems in Europe and Asia.

M. Nicolaus, 'The Unknown Marx', *New Left Review*, no. 48 (1968). Neo-Marxian view of Marx's unfamiliar *Grundrisse*.

C. Posner, *Reflections on the Revolution in France: 1968* (Harmondsworth, Middlesex: Penguin Books, 1970). A collection of essays by some of the participants in the events, more interesting as primary material than as analysis, though Posner's introduction is a useful piece of 'Tourainian' analysis.

N. Poulantzas, *Pouvoir Politique et Classes Sociales* (Paris: Maspéro paperback edition, 1971). An Althusserian view of political power in Marxist theory and capitalist society. The State is the mechanism that co-ordinates the various social 'levels'.

J. A. Raffaele, *Labor Leadership in Italy and Denmark* (Madison, Wisconsin: University of Wisconsin Press, 1962). Useful comparison based on interviews with trade union leaders.

J.-D. Reynaud, S. Dassa, J. Dassa and P. Maclouf, 'Les évènements de mai et juin 1968 et le système français de relations professionnelles', *Sociologie du Travail*, xiii (1971). Locates novelty of the events as lying in a crisis within the industrial enterprise rather than the wider society.

A. M. Ross and P. T. Hartman, *Changing Patterns of Industrial Conflict* (New York: John Wiley, 1960). Classic analysis of international twentieth-century strike rates, relatively free from conventional 'end of ideology' simplifications.

P. Taft, *Organized Labor in American History* (New York: Harper & Row, 1964). A standard work of reference on the decline of extremism and diversity in the U.S. labour movement.

A. Touraine, *La conscience ouvrière* (Paris: Éditions du Seuil, 1966). A bold attempt to generalise about the historical development of the working class on the basis of a cross-sectional study of contemporary French industry.

——, *Le mouvement de mai ou le communisme utopique* (Paris: Éditions du Seuil, 1968). The most interesting acount of May 1968. A serious attempt to link the workers' and students' movements to the structure of post-industrial society.

——, *The Post-Industrial Society*, American edn (New York: Random House, 1971). An interesting though somewhat over-general analysis of modern Western society. The reader may find it difficult to understand unless he has read earlier works by Touraine.

M. Tripier, 'Le revendication des "conseils d'unité" au Comisariat à l'Energie Atomique en mai–juin 1968. Essai d'interprétation', *Revue française de Sociologie*, xi (1970). Empirical support for Touraine—the research process itself made the atomic energy workers more conscious of decision-making processes in the Authority and in the wider society.

L. Trotsky, *History of the Russian Revolution* (London: Sphere Books paperback edition, 1967). Brilliant account of the revolution by one of its main protagonists. Theoretically most interesting for the treatment of uneven development and the role of personality in social change (especially the Romanovs, Kornilov and Lenin).

D. Vidal, 'Idéologies et types d'action syndicale', *Sociologie du Travail*, x (1968). Using same data as Durand (see above), Vidal argues, somewhat obscurely, for the independence of the ideological dimension.

A. Willener, *Interprétation de l'Organisation dans l'Industrie* (Paris: Mouton, 1967). Interviews with workers and management in French iron and steel industry, emphasising the 'action frame of reference'.